Living a Sheltered Life

Living a Sheltered Life

Christian Life Lessons through Homeless Youth

by PAUL CUMMINGS

Foreword by Charles Ringma

RESOURCE *Publications* • Eugene, Oregon

LIVING A SHELTERED LIFE
Christian Life Lessons through Homeless Youth

Copyright © 2019 Paul Cummings. All rights reserved. Except for brief quotations in critical publications or reviews, no part of this book may be reproduced in any manner without prior written permission from the publisher. Write: Permissions, Wipf and Stock Publishers, 199 W. 8th Ave., Suite 3, Eugene, OR 97401.

Resource Publications
An Imprint of Wipf and Stock Publishers
199 W. 8th Ave., Suite 3
Eugene, OR 97401

www.wipfandstock.com

PAPERBACK ISBN: 978-1-7252-5180-9
HARDCOVER ISBN: 978-1-7252-5181-6
EBOOK ISBN: 978-1-7252-5182-3

Manufactured in the U.S.A.   DECEMBER 13, 2019

All Scripture quotations, unless otherwise indicated, are taken from the Holy Bible, New International Version®, NIV®. Copyright ©1973, 1978, 1984, 2011 by Biblica, Inc.™ Used by permission of Zondervan. All rights reserved worldwide. www.zondervan.com The "NIV" and "New International Version" are trademarks registered in the United States Patent and Trademark Office by Biblica, Inc.™

To the homeless youth who taught me so much.
To the team I had around me at Teen Challenge (Brisbane).

Whoever fears the Lord has a secure fortress,
and for their children it will be a refuge. (Proverbs 14:26 NIV)

Contents

Foreword by Charles Ringma | ix
Preface | xi
Acknowledgments | xiii
Introduction | xv

CHAPTER 1   Answered Prayer | 1
CHAPTER 2   First Shift | 6
CHAPTER 3   Things That Go Bump In the Night | 19
CHAPTER 4   Horsing Around | 24
CHAPTER 5   Sally & Norman | 28
CHAPTER 6   Life & Death | 33
CHAPTER 7   Changing Places | 37
CHAPTER 8   Director's Tears | 41
CHAPTER 9   Administration & Communication | 45
CHAPTER 10 Angie | 52
CHAPTER 11 Liar Liar | 58
CHAPTER 12 The Sting | 63
CHAPTER 13 Public Relations | 69
CHAPTER 14 Prayer | 73
CHAPTER 15 Daily Dangers | 76

CHAPTER 16 Make 'em Laugh | 81
CHAPTER 17 Faithful Volunteers | 86
CHAPTER 18 Whinge & Gripe | 90
CHAPTER 19 Outings | 95
CHAPTER 20 Choosing Staff | 100
CHAPTER 21 Lost Child | 105
CHAPTER 22 Stan | 108
CHAPTER 23 Prayer Ending | 113

Foreword

THERE ARE THREE BOOKS.

All are meant to be read, since all are important, even though they are very different.

The book of nature tells us something of God's creativity, beauty and power. It also reminds us of our great responsibility to be careful stewards. So that instead of destroying, we care for the world that God has made. The other book is very different. It's a book of words, not of majestic mountains and terrifying oceans. But these are not any old words. They are special, because they tell the amazing story of how God has made the world, and us, and how he loves us and sent Jesus to make us new and whole. The bible is a wonderful book. It contains the heartbeat of God for us. It shows us what is worth living for and how we can be friends of God and servants of one another. But there is a third kind of book. The book of experience. And that is the kind of book you have in your hands right now. While scripture is God's big picture book, our experience of life and the experiences of others are the little books that only finally make sense when they are read in the light of God's big book. And that is what Paul Cummings has so powerfully done in this series of stories played out in a Brisbane youth shelter. In these brief snippets, these snapshots, you will meet a kaleidoscope of young people and those who seek to provide care and hope. You will meet the lost, the angry, the abused, the misunderstood and the hurting and alienated young people of our affluent yet badly fractured world. But you will meet them in a special

FOREWORD

way. You won't meet them as statistics, Nor as a conglomerate of all that is wrong in our urban world. You will meet them as real characters. Finely portrayed through Paul's sense of detail and humor. But more importantly, these real people with their big story. So this is not a book of mere description but a book of wisdom and of life's important lessons. And if you are tempted to think that this is mere fiction. You are wrong. I was there. Paul's book is ideal as preparation for all who want to work with troubled youth. But it is also suitable for young people reflecting on blessings, challenges and possible pitfalls of making their way into adulthood. Finally, it is a great resource for youth discussion on how God's purpose and plan can impact lives so that we can build the next generation in hope and faith and not in despair and alienation.

—**Dr. Charles Ringma**

Founder of Teen Challenge in Australia. Professor Emeritus, Regent College, Author of Hear the Ancient Wisdom and Of Martyrs, Monks, and Mystics.

Preface

WHEN I FIRST STARTED working with the homeless youth of Australia while working for Teen Challenge (Brisbane), I thought I understood their plight. I was wrong. Homelessness is complex. Many people could never begin to understand the circumstances leading to the homelessness of our youth. That's partly why I have written this book. I've aimed, in simple terms, to convey something of why some of our youth find themselves in emergency circumstances without anywhere to live. It is a fleeting glance of some hundreds of youth who passed my way. It is a chance for the reader to gain something of an understanding of their situation and plight.

I will also share insights God showed me through the youth themselves and how these valuable lessons equipped me for future tasks.

My aim is that Christian's who work with homeless, disadvantaged, or youth at risk, will find the principles God taught me useful for themselves to reflect on and learn from. Many of these principals are born out of hard work, experience, tears, and a large helping of prayer. My real hope is that even a simple book like this may inspire and encourage, at least one person, to positive action for youth at risk, wherever they may be in the world.

The names of the youth have been changed for the sake of protecting their identity. I thank God through my Lord Jesus Christ for the opportunity to share a journey which, for me, was life changing. I hope it will be for others.

—Paul Cummings

Acknowledgments

Chris, for loving and supporting me through the journey.

Charles Ringma, for his example to my life, and writing the foreword.

Jinny L Rodman for her editing skills, insights, and support.

Introduction

EVEN NOW, YEARS LATER, I still remember her face and the emotions I felt, as if it were yesterday.

She seemed so fragile, hunched over in the open doorway with her head bowed. She could not look me in the face. Her eyes could not meet mine, not that they needed to. They darted to and fro around the ground in front of her feet. They could find no rest. Her shoulder length hair hung down and stuck to cheeks, wet from tears. Constantly trying to wipe the hair from her face, the more she tried, the more it seemed to stick. Her crying had now ceased, probably more from exhausting the supply source than having no reason to continue.

She stood trembling between two male police detectives. Silhouetted against the streetlight, the detectives seemed almost embarrassed to be there. After a moment, they confirmed who they were, and just stood there, seemingly not knowing what to do. It was obvious the officers felt as uneasy with the situation as she did. I motioned with my arm and invited them all inside. The detectives declined. They had done their job, made their delivery, and now would be on their way. They mumbled a few words to the girl about how someone would come and see her the next day, and then turned around and walked away. They left like a couple of frightened whippets with their tails between their legs, vanishing beyond the haze of the streetlight.

I had felt uneasy in her company since opening the door. As I led her through to the kitchen, my sense of uneasiness grew until

Introduction

I realized I felt completely out of place. I felt like I had been set up. Just half an hour ago I had received the telephone call, and now here she was, twelve years of age, sexually abused by her father, and alone in my presence. Yes, I felt so deeply out of place. Then again, I figured, who wouldn't?

Just a few hours earlier she had been a normal twelve-year-old girl. Now, ordeal began, she was a quivering mass of helplessness. The police and other helping agencies didn't seem to be too interested at the moment. The police had brought her, but they were off as soon as they could be, and the other so-called helping agencies couldn't seem to be able to get out of bed. I was beginning to feel very angry about the whole situation. My anger wouldn't help her though. The last thing this girl needed was a display of my self-righteous judgement on the rest of the helping services.

I led her through to the kitchen and seated her at the dining table. "Cuppa?" I asked. She just kept looking down and shrugged her shoulders. I put the kettle on while pondering the fact that there would be many other helping agencies working that night. I supposed they must be busy, and anyway the police couldn't be expected to be all things to all people, their job was difficult enough as it was. My anger dispersed a little.

It was 3:00 a.m., and normally, if someone came in at this time I would put them straight to bed, but I sensed this girl needed some time to adjust to her new environment. I felt like a fish out of water floundering on the beach. After all, I was only a volunteer, I had no special skills for dealing with such situations, apart from prayer, that is. I could hardly begin to wonder what she must be feeling. Silently within, I was praying for God to help me out in this situation, and that he might somehow make everything work out all right for this girl, and that she would be comforted in some way.

Normally, I could tell a joke or two or more, and the kids usually liked that, but this was not the time for frivolity. A hand on the shoulder could sometimes be edifying, but there was no way I was going to touch this girl at all. She was too traumatised from being

Introduction

"touched" earlier in the evening. Ideally, there would have been a female worker with me who would have been better suited to this type of situation. However, lack of finances and an acute shortage of female volunteers prevented this from being the case.

I jumped up to turn off the kettle, "Tea or coffee?" Again, she just shrugged her shoulders and said nothing. I made two coffees and put milk and sugar on the table, and pushed one of the coffees in front of her. She turned her head away, ever so slightly, as if in rejection of the drink, then returned her head to its original position with a look of guilt, as if to apologize for moving it in the first place. I fixed up my milk and sugar, putting each of them closer to her when I had finished. Not knowing what to say I just sat there sipping my drink. The silence was deafening.

Eventually, she helped herself to milk and sugar. I apologized for having raw sugar instead of nice clean white sugar that most people I knew were familiar with. I explained that I didn't like that particular sugar, but the people who did the household shopping did. Not the greatest of conversations, but at least it was something. This comment must have amused her, as a faint smile came to her face, even though her eyes still looked down.

I thought I'd take this opportunity to explain to her where the bathroom and bedrooms were. I didn't consider it worthwhile to begin talking to her of her traumatic experience; there would be others more qualified than myself to do that some other time. There were forms to fill out and details to gather, but I considered they could wait until the morning. The morning, I thought, is not too far away, and this girl needs sleep. I knew it would be a difficult and traumatic day ahead for her, and she would need all the sleep she could get. I suggested I could show her to the girl's bedroom, as she was looking very tired. She nodded a polite approval and sat up in her chair ready to follow me.

As I came back from the girl's room, I couldn't help thinking how helpless I felt. I wish I could have done more. But what? The needs encountered at the shelter always seemed so vast that often I felt it was a waste of time being there. However, the first lesson

Introduction

I learnt was that being there was what it was all about. Someone needed to be.

I left early for work the next morning, before any of the kids were out of bed. I never saw the girl again. But I can still see her face.

CHAPTER 1

Answered Prayer

> Commit to the LORD whatever you do,
> and he will establish your plans. (Proverbs 16:3 NIV)

"Who's on the 'phone?"

The words broke through my thoughts and brought me back to reality. The telephone call was finished, but I had not hung up the receiver before embarking on a trip down memory lane of my days as a volunteer at Hebron House, an emergency and short-term youth emergency accommodation center, run by Teen Challenge in Brisbane. My wife Christine (Chris) had caught me deep in thought. As I replaced the receiver, I was amazed how thoughts from years before could be so vivid. "It was Claude. There's a job listed at Hebron, part-time and with pay. He thought I might be interested." Claude was the Executive Director of Teen Challenge, as well as Chris's personal friend.

My thoughts automatically returned to my days as a volunteer. Would I really want to go back to sleeping away from home, eating substandard food, putting up with abuse from kids, parents, and, at times, other workers? Would I really want to spend all night policing residents, use steam irons which kids have urinated in, become physically, mentally, and emotionally worn out? The prospect seemed daunting to say the least, but at least I knew what I would be getting myself into. Chris interrupted my thought again with, "That sounds great, it's an answer to prayer." Fortunately, she could not have been reading my thoughts, but I had to confess that it did seem like the perfect answer to prayer.

I had just left work, after nine years at the same job, to go to Bible College. A few people thought I was being pretty stupid, leaving a good steady job with the Brisbane City Council to go to Bible College, of all places. I could understand them thinking that my decision may not have seemed logical, but then sometimes following God by faith does not always seem to be logical to the natural mind. Chris and I had decided that I would go to college part-time and, if possible, work part-time. Chris had a job, but a little extra income to cover my college fees would be helpful. Just two days before Claude's call, we had been very specific in prayer to the Lord. We asked for a part-time job in a Christian organization, with pay. Such opportunities are few and far between, but we felt it was all right to ask. So Claude's call seemed the obvious answer to our prayer.

The next day, I telephoned Claude to let him know I was interested in applying for the position. He said he needed to contact the director of Hebron and would get back to me. A few moments later the telephone rang. It was Claude with the details. First of all, he asked me if I knew Alec, the director of Hebron, which I didn't. This seemed to surprise Claude because when he had mentioned my name to Alec, his response was to ask if I was a guy with a bald head wearing glasses, to which Claude told him I was. I just assumed Alec must have heard of me or seen me somewhere. At the time, I thought no more about it. I was to be interviewed that afternoon.

As I drove up to the new Hebron, compared to the old one I had known, it looked wonderful. Though it had kept the same name, Hebron had changed location since I had worked there as a volunteer. I parked the car and admired the beautiful white old Queenslander styled house nestled under a couple of enormous mango trees, both fully laden with fruit. The shade from the trees fell down over the house and together with the surrounding shrubs the whole scene looked quite idyllic. As I walked up the front steps and knocked on the large double doors, I wondered just what it would feel like working in a shelter again.

A young man in his early twenties opened the door, when I saw his face I knew immediately what it would be like to work in a shelter again. He looked exhausted! There were bags under his eyes, and he looked unkempt. It looked like it was a struggle for him to keep standing; it seemed on a first appearance that he was a picture of total fatigue. However, with a compassionate tone in his voice, he asked if he could help me. I explained why I was there, so he invited me in and introduced himself as David. His sincere and gentle manner impressed me. David led me through the veranda, the hall and kitchen and into the dining area, where he fixed me up with a cup of tea, made a brief apology and left me alone. Later, I would discover it was his job I was applying for.

I sat there making comparisons between this house and the old shelter. In this house the main living space was one long open plan room with four designated areas. From my vantage point in the dining area, I could see through the kitchen and pool table area and down to the living room section. I considered this a distinct advantage, compared with the old place. In the old shelter, when you were in the kitchen, things would go bump in the combined living room and pool table area, but whenever you rushed out to see what the problem was, the kids would all be sitting on the sofa politely chatting and acting as if they had no idea anything had happened. This seemed to happen often. Probably, the one I remember most, was rushing from the kitchen into the living room after hearing the sound of smashing glass, only to find kids sitting, watching TV oblivious of the window that had just been broken. Yes, there were distinct advantages to this new setting.

Suddenly, there was a hand thrust out towards me. Alec had appeared from the office and, in just a couple of steps, was face to face with me. We shook hands and introduced ourselves and wandered into the office. It struck me immediately that Alec was quite a dynamic person. You could tell from looking at him that he was under severe stress and tired, but he seemed to move and talk with a sense of purpose, in a very direct and straightforward manner. He looked young, and later I was to discover, he was only twenty years of age. I was taken by the fact that he seemed very mature for his age.

The office, compared to the rest of the house, was very dingy and dark; the lighting was just not adequate. It was quite a large room with just one small light from the ceiling and two lamps on one end of the room. We moved to the end of the room with the lamps and sat on some old cane furniture, which at the time, I thought seemed to suit the house. Alec handed me an application form for the vacant position and explained he would interview me after I had completed it. In the dim light, I filled out the form, with some difficulty in seeing, and handed it back to him. Then came the questions.

I felt the interview went very well; I sensed the fact that I had worked at Hebron before was in my favor, plus a few years before, I had taken twelve months leave without pay from my work at the council and done a training course with Teen Challenge. It was the first interview in a long time that I felt at ease within myself. I had been to a few interviews when considering other positions over the previous twelve months, and although I could have taken other jobs, I never felt right in the interviews. This interview was different. By the time we had finished I knew I wanted this job, not just because of the money, but because I knew within myself God had given me the gifts and talents to do it.

Alec must also have thought as I did because he offered me the job on the spot. I told him I wanted the job, but as it would involve being away from home three nights every two weeks, I would have to discuss the hours with my wife first. We parted with the agreement that I would get back to him within the next few days.

Chris and I both felt right about the hours and the job, but decided to talk to the elders from church before contacting Alec again. We had consulted with the elders about leaving my previous employment, and we thought it wise to consult them on this

Answered Prayer

as well because my work hours would, at times, conflict with my church commitments. There was no problem from the elders, so I called Alec and confirmed my starting date, which happened to be on my birthday. It was to be a birthday I would never forget, and I would soon find out why Alec had asked Claude if I had a bald head and wore spectacles.

CHAPTER 2

First Shift

Deliver me from my enemies, O God;
Be my fortress against those who are attacking me. (Psalm 59:1 NIV)

MY SHIFTS AT THE shelter were to be every Monday and every other weekend.

Monday mornings at Hebron House, I discovered, were not a pretty sight. Well, most of them anyway. All the issues and dramas of the weekend would build up, and there was an immediate need to prioritize and work through everything. Since Alec didn't officially work on the weekends, it was often a mammoth task for him to sort everything out on Monday. The task was not made any easier by the fact that the staff who had been working the weekends were not always around or able to be contacted on Mondays. There were power struggles between the kids to sort out, staff decisions to analyze, Child Care Officers to contact, Police to notify, parents to call, a house to tidy, shopping to do, the list could go on and on. Alec would take each child into the office, one at a time, and work on their case.

As it was my first day, I was not familiar with the new ways of Hebron House. There was not a lot I could do without guidance from Alec, but at least my previous volunteer work at the old Hebron helped me to relate to the kids. I watched over the remaining residents, whilst making sure breakfast dishes and a bit of house tidying was done, while waiting for Alec to finish. The morning grew into afternoon as rapidly as the afternoon grew into evening, with Alec attempting to instruct, in between his non-stop workload. Alec and I prayed together just before he left, and I was under strict instructions to contact him on his pager if there were any problems.

I'd made a nice meal of mashed potatoes, vegetables and sausages to be followed by ice cream and canned fruit. It was a real challenge having to cook for eight children and three adults, especially since I was used to my wife doing the majority of our cooking at home. Generally, Hebron prepared for up to eight residents; however, occasionally we would have extra if there were emergencies. For my first night, we were full, and Chris was coming over to be with me as it was my birthday. I also had a volunteer coming, named Kim, who I had never met.

The quality of some volunteers left a lot to be desired. Though they were always appreciated, they could sometimes put you in difficult situations. As I pondered on what type of volunteer Kim might be, I couldn't help but remember Trish.

Even though I had only been a volunteer at the old Hebron House, I had shown enough initiative to be left in charge sometimes. I usually had a female volunteer working with me. Trish became a volunteer who was often scheduled to work with me, and we had many laughs together, though we did not always see eye to eye.

As much as we worked well together, Trish did put me in some difficult situations without really trying. I remembered one evening in particular. It was after lights out and all the residents were in bed, except for one young man who had not arrived home by curfew. I was pretty tired, and Trish said she would wait up so I could go to bed. I had been working at my job all day and had come straight to Hebron after work, which meant I had been on the go since 6:30 a.m., and it was now nearly midnight. I had an early start the next morning, too.

As I snuggled into bed, I remember thinking I would quickly fall asleep. Nothing could have been further from the truth. As soon as my head hit the pillow, I could hear Trish talking to someone in the office. I thought it must be the guy who was late coming home, and I seemed to sense all was not well with him. I was soon to find out it was him, and all definitely was not well.

He had come home looking for Tony, the then director, who had been the day worker, to accuse him of splitting up his relationship with his girlfriend. His intention was to confront Tony, and then beat him up. Trish explained to him that Tony was no longer there, but that I was here and pointed him in the direction of my bedroom. Great for Trish, not so great for me. Fortunately, I had already begun to pray for wisdom and even more fortunately I received it.

Suddenly there was silence, and the next thing I knew my bedroom door flew open and crashed against the wall. "Are you Paul Cummings!?," screamed the voice. Now that in itself was not too bad, but as he was screaming, he pulled up his loose hanging t-shirt and proceeded to draw two bits of wood from the inside of his pants. These same bits of wood happened to be joined together with a chain which turned them into a potentially lethal martial arts weapon. He spun them around his body, as I had seen Bruce Lee do in some of his movies, and I could tell this guy had a fair idea of what he was doing. I suspected he had an even better idea of what he was going to do to me. I pulled back the bed covers and leapt to my feet while screaming back at him, "Am I Paul Cummings? Am I Paul Cummings? Never mind if I am Paul Cummings, who are you?!" I made sure to show no fear and that my voice was a couple of decibels higher than his to give a good effect.

I had not yet met this young man, and it was still my assumption, at this point in time, that this was our resident arriving home late. He seemed stunned, and he just stared at me in disbelief, his weapon now dangling limp and aimless by his side. He tried to talk but could only manage to mumble, "I'm staying here."

I was in the process of frantically trying to pull my pants on, and it seemed that I was in control of the situation for the moment, and I thought I'd better keep it that way. I screamed back at him again, "Staying here? Staying here? I'll decide if you're staying here!" I can't say he was a perfect angel after that, but at least no one was hurt, and I felt much better trying to get to sleep knowing his Kung Fu weapon was locked away. However, I did ask Trish to be a little more considerate of me in the future.

I was hoping Kim would not be that type of volunteer. The kids were getting a little impatient for tea and we were still waiting for two boys and for Kim and Chris to arrive. Chris arrived a few moments later with a brightly wrapped parcel under her arm, I couldn't see the point really, I knew it was a pair of jeans, why waste the money on fancy packaging? But Chris liked to do that type of thing.

Kim arrived just as I was about to serve tea, we said a brief hello and went straight into feeding the hungry masses. The two male residents had not arrived home yet, but they knew what time tea was served, anyway, we would save them some.

Meal times always seemed to bring out the worst in the residents, though it could also be a great time to get to know some of them more closely. I looked in horror as my beautifully prepared food was soaked, saturated, and then rolled in what seemed to be an ever-flowing river of ketchup. The bottle was the biggest I had ever seen and, as someone who rarely uses the mixture, I found it all quite sickening to watch. As time went by, I began to learn that to Hebron residents, ketchup was the opiate which made all meals taste good.

I had to leave the meal table a number of times to answer the telephone. Each time it was the same person, the brother of one of the female residents staying there. I had been instructed to expect him to call, but under no circumstances was I to let his sister speak to him. Why she couldn't speak to her own brother I wasn't sure, only Alec had that information. I did know she was on a "Form Four" from the Department of Family Services which meant that while she was in our care we were classed as her legal guardian, that meant she was supposed to do as we requested.

As I returned to the table, the telephone rang again. Kim must have seen my frustration and volunteered to answer it. I finished my tea, and by now it was just Chris and I at the table, as the residents never hung around long after the food was gone. As I was leaving the table, Kim popped her head around the corner and asked me if I could spare a moment in the office. I asked Chris to keep an eye on the residents and joined Kim.

If I thought the office was dark and dingy in the daylight hours, it was nothing compared to the evening. Kim informed me Miranda's brother (Miranda was the girl on the "Form Four") had telephoned again and he was on his way over.

The news had not really taken me by surprise, as I half expected that to be his next move. Hebron was not really that hard to find, as we wanted kids with nowhere to live to be able to find it easily. We knew he could find the address in the telephone book and we considered that if he was calling from Miranda's normal home address and if he was leaving right then by car, then he could be at Hebron within the next ten minutes.

Alec had asked me to page him if there were any problems, and I thought I had better do so, just to cover myself. I was later to discover that it could sometimes take quite a while to receive a call from Alec after paging him, fortunately tonight though, his response was swift. I spoke with Alec and my instructions were straight forward, don't let the brother in the house, don't let him talk to Miranda, and keep an eye on Miranda so she doesn't run off with him if she sees him outside.

As I hung up the telephone, I explained the instructions to Kim. We decided to pray and hand the whole situation over to the Lord, and I'm sure glad we did. We decided that Kim would casually keep an eye on Miranda, and I would keep myself free to be able to answer the door. It was not long before our strategy began to go horribly wrong.

Kim was in the living room talking with Miranda and two other female residents, while Chris was talking to another girl on

First Shift

the deck outside, and I was chatting to one of the male residents about the importance of holding a pool cue correctly. Suddenly the back door flew open. I thought it must be the brother wanting to take us by surprise, but to my relief, in walked the two male residents who were late coming home for tea. My relief quickly turned to anguish when I realized they were both drunk! The house rules were such that if anyone came home drunk, they had to be evicted. However, this decision had to be made by the director, so this meant another paging of Alec.

Fortunately, the two boys were not disruptive, as they knew they were on thin ice and were in danger of having nowhere decent to sleep that night. I left them in the dining area with their tea and went into the office to page Alec. No sooner had I picked up the telephone, even before I had time to dial the number, I heard a fearful scream and the next thing I knew Kim bolted into the office. "He's in the house" said Kim, referring to Miranda's brother, then looking down sheepishly, she continued, "And he's talking to Miranda."

It wasn't really Kim's fault; situations rarely seemed to turn out as you would want them to at Hebron. Some wise person once said, "If anything can go wrong, it will." I think that person must have worked at Hebron at some time. You see, unfortunately for us, the female residents restroom is out on the veranda next to the main entry door. Normally, this would not be a problem, however in this little scenario, its location was of strategic importance. One of the girls had gone to the restroom, and on her way back to the living room noticed someone at the front door. Thinking she was doing the right thing, she let the person in and asked him to wait on the veranda; the person happened to be Miranda's brother. As the girl continued on her way, whom should she pass on her way to the living room but Miranda, who was on her way to the restroom. Of course, the mighty scream was let out by Miranda, as she saw her brother standing there. It was only later in the evening, as Kim and I analyzed the events that I understood what had happened.

As for now, it was panic stations, and I rushed from the office through the hallway to the veranda, not really knowing what

I might find. Fearful images of a battered Miranda or worse still, no Miranda at all, were flashing through my mind, not to mention trying to explain the whole sorry affair to Alec. Once on the veranda, my initial fears were removed as I saw the two of them sitting on the old couch facing each other and talking quietly. Miranda had her back to me, so I went over and stood in a position where I could see her face, she seemed all right, there were no tears and more importantly, no blood.

I felt frustrated with the lack of information regarding them. Why weren't they allowed to be together? Could he harm her? Could she harm him? Was he a psychopath? There were just so many possibilities I decided to discount them all, rather than allow myself to become paranoid. I determined to just do my job and deal with the situation as it unfolded.

I held out my hand to the brother and introduced myself, he stood and shook my hand, "I'm Peter, Miranda's brother," he said in a soft voice. His handshake was firm and, together with his broad smile, it appeared on the surface that he was genuinely pleased to meet me. While he presented well, I knew there was no way I was going to turn my back on this guy. Earlier in the evening, he had abused both Kim and me on the telephone, and now in meeting me he was acting as if nothing had happened. I thought I'd give him an opportunity to redeem himself with me and said, "Are you the brother I spoke to three or four times on the telephone earlier this evening?" He told me that it had been him and just kept on smiling. I proceeded to do my job.

I explained to him clearly and precisely that I had received instructions that, Miranda was now in the care of the Department of Family Services, and that while she stayed with us we were her legal guardian. I went on to explain that I had been informed not to let him see or speak with Miranda, and therefore he would have to leave the premises immediately.

In fairy tales, frogs are turned into princes, here I think I was turning a prince into a frog. The countenance of this prince charming changed immediately, and though he was probably turning a bright shade of red, he did look somewhat green in the dismal lighting. He looked like he was getting ready to explode. Miranda must have noticed the change because she left her seat and stood with Kim, who was watching proceedings from the hall doorway. I felt as if I was maybe being a bit too hard on the guy, but I had to do my job and this is what I had been told to do. The way I saw it, I was there to protect the residents, and if that meant being hard on some people, then hard I had to be. I thought I'd make my next move before he made his, so I moved to my left and caught hold of the front door latch and opened the door. "Out please, Peter," I said firmly. The rage seemed to subside from his face, and he took on a look of bewilderment, as his eyes glanced back and forth between Miranda, myself, and the doorway. He never said anything, but moved towards Miranda. I overtook him and stood between them. He stopped as his chest met mine, I was determined not to move and was silently asking the Lord for strength and wisdom to handle the situation. I believed the Lord could work it out before things became too out of hand. I could see in his eyes that here was a man who was full of anger and frustration and yet I felt he didn't have the inner fortitude to start anything too serious for fear of getting himself hurt.

We were both around the same size but I think deep inside he knew I was determined to do my job and that to get past me to his sister was not going to be easy. I never entered a situation like this with the thought of fighting with or hurting anyone. In reality, I probably couldn't have fought my way out of a wet paper bag, but there was one thing in my favor, could I be stubborn! "Out!" I said.

He just kept looking me in the eye with his chest against mine, in an effort to show he wasn't scared of me, but I suspected that he was. Still looking him in the eye, I asked Kim to call the police. Kim went into the office to make the call.

He mumbled something about me hiding behind the police, turned, and started to walk towards the front door. As he reached the door, he looked around to Miranda, his face was now like that of a lost little boy searching for a friend. "Come with me Miranda. You know I love you." Miranda tried to push past me, but I held her back with my right arm while I pointed to the door with my left arm, "Get out, now!" Surprisingly he stepped out of the door, I think he only did it to entice Miranda outside. By now, I was holding onto her with both arms and she was struggling to get out of my hold. I'd seen enough to suspect there was more to their relationship than met the eye, possibly some form of abuse from her brother or maybe even incest. There wasn't any way I was going to let Miranda go.

Kim reappeared on the scene and frantically closed and bolted the door. Miranda fell in a heap on the ground and started crying. Kim and I helped her up and led her into the office. In the office, we could hear the brother outside calling Miranda's name and asking her to go with him. Fortunately, at this point, Miranda didn't seem too interested in going anywhere, and made no moves to get to her brother. In fact, she looked up and said, "Get rid of him!" I was pleased with her idea, but I didn't know if I could comply.

I left Kim and Miranda in the office and proceeded to check on the rest of the household. Although I hadn't really wanted her to come along that evening, Chris was turning out to be a real asset. She had organized supper for the kids, seen to it that the other three female residents had their showers and were ready for bed, and had two of the male residents lined up for their showers. The two drunks were blissfully asleep on their beds, on the top of their bed sheets, fully clothed. I figured I would just have to deal with them later.

The police had not turned up yet, so I decided to confront the brother through a window rather than go outside. We exchanged words for about five minutes, with me asking him to leave and with him shouting obscenities back at me. It was about 10:00 p.m. by now, and apart from the obvious, all seemed very quiet in the neighborhood. I was surprised no disgusted neighbors came out to abuse the both of us. He must have come over to the house by taxi, because when he did finally leave, he ran along the road and up the hill. Apparently, he was going home to get his shotgun and come back and shoot me.

The police had not arrived yet, so I called them to let them know that the problem had passed and that we would not need their services. By now, Miranda was having her shower, and Chris was making Kim and I some supper with a hot drink.

The male residents were beginning to make a bit of noise in their bedroom, so I went in to quiet them down. The two who had been drinking were called Shaun and Shane, and they were beginning to pay for their excess of supposed pleasure. So were the other two residents, the household property and very shortly myself. Shaun (or was it Shane, I always got their names mixed up) had vomited all over himself and his bed.

The boy's room was not large, and consisted of four narrow cupboards around six feet high with one piece louvered doors, which were used as wardrobes. There were two sets of bunk beds in the room as well. The floors were bare, wooden floors, with a few rugs spread around here and there. Shaun had been lying on one of the bottom bunks when he vomited. This was probably a good thing, as he would have sprayed the whole room from a higher vantage point. They must have drowned their sorrows earlier in the evening with a mixture of beer and rum, which was obvious from the stench around the room.

As I dragged Shaun off of the bed and into the general direction of the toilet bowl, my initial feeling was one of anger. How could these guys go out and get drunk, knowing it would jeopardize their living situation? I asked myself over and over. I went on to wonder just what goes through the mind of a couple of sixteen year old kids to warrant doing this sort of thing. Surely they could have more sense! Surely they would understand the consequences! Surely they would know better!

I was glad the toilet was just outside the boy's room as Shaun wasn't offering much assistance in getting there, and he was quite a big boy to be dragging across the floor. Finally, in position over the toilet bowl I encouraged Shaun to stick his fingers down his throat and vomit up all that he could. He complied with my request admirably. As I was kneeling there holding him, I continued to question the sanity of the young men in my care.

As would happen often in my work at Hebron House, when I became judgmental or began to question things, the Holy Spirit would begin to speak to me. First of all came the scripture from the book of Romans which says, "You, therefore, have no excuse, you who pass judgment on someone else, for at whatever point you judge another, you are condemning yourself, because you who pass judgement do the same things," (Romans 2:1 NIV). Immediately following the scripture, my mind was flooded with memories of when I was fifteen, of how two nights in a row I had managed to get myself drunk on alcoholic cider, and that even now, because of that time, the smell of someone else drinking alcoholic cider would make me want to vomit. I always found it a blessing in my time at Hebron, how the Lord would deal with my inner thoughts and feelings, and change my thoughts and attitudes towards the kids and the situations I faced.

I looked at Shaun with different eyes. No longer was he just some stupid kid who should know better. Now he was a person with every bit as much worth as I. He was now as I had been all those years earlier, drunk and needing a friend. Where would I have been if my friends had forsaken me, worse still, what would have become of me if my family had rejected me, like Shaun's family had rejected him.

I helped him to his feet and suggested he have a shower. The idea seemed good to him, probably because the shower was next to the toilet bowl and he would not have far to walk.

I went to get him a change of clothes and returned a few moments later with the clothes in one hand and Shane in the other. Shane had not yet vomited, but I was taking no chances and positioned him over the toilet bowl; it didn't take long before his cocktail was re-introducing itself.

Eventually, both of them had been showered and changed for bed. I had to put a different mattress on Shaun's bed and remake it, and strangely enough the task had not been too overwhelming for me. I think I now felt I was doing it for a fellow traveller and not just some stupid street kid.

The whole affair had seemed a minor incident really, and yet, I was a changed man because of it. The best part was that I had a real peace about the whole situation, not just dealing with the residents getting drunk, but a sort of confirmation that I was where God wanted me to be.

I said good night to all the male residents, turned out the light in their bedroom, closed the door, and went to the office to join Chris and Kim. Chris and Kim had been on hand to help with the boys if I needed them, but I'd told them to have their supper and I would join them later. As I walked in the office, Chris greeted me with a cup of tea and a piece of buttered bun.

"Do you think he'll return?" asked Chris. The ladies had obvious concerns regarding the return of Miranda's brother. "Always possible I suppose, but I doubt it myself. My guess is he would be too scared of getting into serious trouble."

Hebron policy was to pray at the end of each shift. I suggested we do that before we had any further interruptions. We had been praying for about five minutes when the telephone rang; it was Miranda's brother. Very politely he asked if he could speak to Miranda, I explained she was asleep and was unavailable to talk to him (I couldn't be bothered explaining yet again that he wasn't allowed to talk to her anyway). He thanked me, and hung up. I shook my head in disbelief at his perseverance and sudden attack of manners. I rejoined the girls in prayer.

Our prayer time was pretty simple and consisted mainly of asking the Lord for protection for ourselves, the house and kids, and from anything Miranda's brother might do. As it was well after midnight, Kim went straight to bed after our prayer time, as she had to leave at 7:00 a.m. to catch her bus for work. There would be time for me to get to know her better in the weeks ahead. My first impressions of Kim were good ones, and these were to prove correct over the coming months we worked together.

I checked all the doors and made sure they were locked and bolted. Chris and I then retired to bed. This was not much fun for me. The male staff bedroom consisted of one single bed. This was to be for Chris, and I was on the floor. As we conversed in the darkness, it seemed quite funny to us as we thought back over the night we had just experienced. Chris had come to spend time with me on my birthday, however, ironically, she had hardly even seen or spoken with me throughout the night.

We wondered if Peter would return, however, the thought must not have been too threatening to us because we immediately drifted off to sleep. What a birthday! What a first shift!

CHAPTER 3

Things That Go Bump In the Night

Save me, O God, by your name:
vindicate me by your might.(Psalm 54:1 NIV)

I SAT UP STARTLED. Something had awoken me, but I was not sure what. I rested my head on the pillow and listened intently. Chris was not awake, but that was not unusual for her. I reckoned sleeping was her hobby. Nothing could stir her, once she was asleep. Thud! There it was again. It sounded like a half brick landing on the roof. The old Queenslander had a tin roof which really magnified the sound of anything hitting it. I discovered later that sometimes during heavy rainfall the noise of rain hitting the roof was so intense you could hardly hear yourself speak, or even think for that matter. I checked the time on my watch; I think it was the first time in my life I'd found the need to use the night light built into the watch. It read 3:00 a.m.

Could it be Peter returning to shoot me, or maybe some kids throwing rocks on the roof out of spite or trying to gain the attention of one of the residents? I proceeded to leave my sleeping spot and go and check around the house. I had a flashlight handy, but decided not to turn it on for fear of giving away my position to any would be intruder or attacker. I regretted my decision, as I bashed my knee against the coffee table and stubbed my toe on the office desk, fumbling to find the doorway to the Recreation room. Thud! There it was yet again! Hitting the roof with a similar intensity as the others.

The sound seemed to come from the other side of the house, so I moved through the pool table area and kitchen into the dining area. There it was again, but now it seemed to be on the opposite side of the house. I moved to the living room window and slowly pulled the curtain back, and looked out onto the street. I couldn't see anyone. I then looked out of the veranda window, and I didn't see anyone there either. I checked the main entrance, moved back to the dining area, and there seemed to be no movement anywhere. During this time, there were three or four further missile attacks in quick succession.

I proceeded to turn on the outside house lights, keeping my head low, as I moved from one side of the house to the other. If Peter was there with a gun waiting for me, I didn't see any point in making myself an easy target for him. This situation didn't feel like a gun situation. Why not just blow the lock off the door and walk in, if you had a gun? This felt more like kids playing around, but you could never be sure what might happen at Hebron. I saw something move outside, in the undergrowth next to the deck. I stood and watched for what seemed an age; no further movement occurred. A couple more thuds on the roof didn't encourage me at all.

I was beginning to feel cranky and a little tired of the situation. I decided I would go outside and have a look. Slowly, and as quietly as possible, I slid open the door to the deck area. I moved out onto the deck and stood there motionless, my back against the wall, wondering what to do next. And then I saw it. One had fallen just a few feet away from me and I had seen it quite clearly. Glinting in the moonlight as it sped earthward I had been able to follow the course of this meaningless missile. I shook my head and smiled to myself. Had I really been out of bed at three in the morning for this? They were all around on the ground, their sweet odor filling the warm humid air. Mangoes! I had been the victim of a cruel practical joke by the mango trees! Ripe mangoes fall off mango trees, and hit roofs, as simple as that. I did a brief check around the property, and then returned to my less than cozy sleeping spot on the floor.

I awoke at 7:00 a.m., and began the day in a manner that was to become my routine over the coming months. Firstly, I would put the telephone onto the answering machine, this was for two reasons. If the phone rang while I was in the shower, the machine obviously would answer it. This would also mean that the phone would hopefully, not ring long enough to wake up any of the residents from their beauty sleep. All of this meant that I would be able to have a shower without any interruptions.

After setting the answer machine, I proceeded to the bathroom for my shower. A great advantage in having a shower at this time of the day meant that no one else was using water at the same time. This usually meant that the water temperature stayed the same. Knowing the foibles of plumbing, though seemingly insignificant in itself, could be of value to a youth worker. For instance, when a resident would use an excessively long shower as a ploy to avoid going to bed, all I had to do was turn on the hot water in the kitchen. If the resident was in the shower, they would vacate the position pretty quickly, as their water supply would turn cold. There were usually loud protests at this point in time, which confirmed the culprit was in the shower. If there were no protests, I then knew that the resident was not in the shower at all, but just trying to waste time. I saw many a puzzled face leave that bathroom, wondering just how I knew they were not in the shower.

After finishing in the bathroom, I would put the kettle on the gas stove and set the dining table for breakfast. The time it took to set the table seemed to coincide with the kettle coming to a boil. I'd grab a cuppa and my Bible, and find a spot somewhere to read and pray. All this happened pretty quickly, and by 7:30 a.m., I would begin to get the kids out of bed.

Living a Sheltered Life

I found that by keeping to this particular routine, my days at Hebron began with a sense of direction and purpose. No matter how difficult the previous twenty-four hours had been, this was a new day, and I would treat it as such. It also set me free in the mornings to concentrate on the kids and their needs, rather than worrying about my own.

Chris and the kids joined me at the breakfast table. Kim had left for work early, which would be her usual routine. Breakfast finished, everyone was assigned a household duty. As well as having to make their own beds, the residents had to do daily chores which included such things as, washing up the dishes, cleaning the bathroom, vacuuming, etc. etc. It was not an easy task to assign the duties, but once allocated, everyone got on with their work.

Alec arrived to a house full of enterprising young cleaners, busily working away. He had a surprised look on his face as he watched everyone, and eventually sauntered into the office with, what appeared to be a contented grin. I said goodbye to Chris, as she left for work, and joined Alec in the office.

Paul, the incoming youth worker, had just arrived and had a look of shock on his face. I was to discover that the looks of surprise and shock from Alec and Paul were due to my early and efficient organizing of the kids. I thought this would be normal, but apparently it wasn't.

The telephone rang. It was Miranda's brother. Rather than hold up our meeting I just told him plainly, "I am sorry but you are not allowed to speak with Miranda." He began to argue so I continued, "As I have repeatedly been telling you since yesterday evening, I do not intend to have to explain myself all over again and I will hang up the phone after I have finished this sentence." After which I hung up the phone. I switched the phone onto the answer machine and sat down opposite Alec and Paul.

The idea of this time together was to hand over from the outgoing staff to the incoming staff. Almost emotionlessly and without warning, Alec began to open the meeting with prayer. His emotions changed as he began to pray and I recall being impressed with his sense of purpose in prayer. He prayed like he knew God

Things That Go Bump In the Night

well. Paul spoke a few words of prayer also, and though his style of prayer was different than Alec's, I could tell he had a heart after God.

"This ministry is based on prayer. Without it, we may as well pack up and go home" said Alec. I would soon discover that when Alec had something to say, he was pretty straight forward in telling you. Having been raised a Yorkshire man with a blunt mouth, I appreciated this particular quality of Alec's personality.

Alec suggested I recall the events of the previous evening. He was very particular to point out that I inform them of the facts of what had occurred, rather than my assumptions of what had happened. As I recalled the evening's events, I really felt put on the spot. But it was good. As I shared, Alec and Paul interjected with pertinent questions to draw out the finer points of what had happened. The more relevant the information I gave them, the better position they would be in to make worthwhile decisions on the matters in hand. Though I had not gone by the "book", I knew from their responses I must have done all right. Alec summed up the facts and suggested it had been a good night's work. He then closed the meeting in prayer.

As he drove me to the railway station, Alec shared how he knew I would be the right person for the job. I was curious to know more, so I enquired, "Claude said when you heard my name you asked if I had a bald head and wore spectacles. Had you seen or heard of me from somewhere else?" I was intrigued to hear his answer. "No!" He said abruptly, while at the same time becoming visibly excited. "It was through prayer. God gave me an image of the person who would fill the job vacancy; someone who was bald and wearing glasses."

Journeying home, as I sat in the train watching the world stream past, I felt a certain contentment in my soul. I knew I was where God wanted me to be!

CHAPTER 4

Horsing Around

Then God said, "Let us make mankind in our image, in our likeness; So that they may rule over the fish in the sea, and the birds in the sky, over the livestock and all the wild animals . . ." (Genesis 1:26 NIV)

IT CERTAINLY DID NOT seem like a good idea to me. Alec had decided to allow the kids to go horseback riding. How we could afford it, I did not know. But Alec was the one making the decisions, and so if it was okay with him, it was okay with me. It was mainly one of the residents, Simon who wanted to go, but it was going to be an outing for the whole house. Except for Alec. Maybe now was the time to tell him I was timid of horses? Maybe not. I'd be okay. God would protect me, wouldn't he? I loaded the kids into the bus, and off we zoomed.

Alec had arranged a special price for us, which I mentioned to the stable manager when we arrived. We must have got a low fee, as the horses we were given seemed like cheap ones. They looked the worse for wear and did not appear to have much energy. The proprietor assured me that once they were in the riding area, they would come to life. I was soon to regret his statement.

Horsing Around

While I was pretty timid and did not really want to ride a horse, I decided to have a go, to be one with the kids. I quickly discovered we were not on the same level. As soon as we mounted the horses, the kids took off with horses running. I was off and panicking. The problem was a simple one, horses like to play follow the leader. At least, on this day they did. We were in a fenced paddock, around an acre in size. Within the confines of the paddock was one solitary jump. This normally would not be a problem to me, because, for one thing I would never usually mount a horse, and for the other thing, now that I was on a horse I would not be stupid enough to go near a jump. Unfortunately, the horse was not in tune with my thoughts, and had thoughts of its own.

Simon was proving to be a quite accomplished rider, which was good to see. It was no wonder he had wanted to come horseback riding. The other kids did not seem as comfortable or confident on a horse, but being teenagers, excuse the pun, they went along for the ride. I went along because it was my job, and I think my horse was now going along because it was its job.

Simon's horse started to canter, so did mine. Simon's horse started to gallop, so did mine. Simon's horse started to head for the jump, so did mine! Now being prepared to mount a horse for the sake of my job seemed reasonable, but to take on a jump? Well, this certainly was not part of any contract I wanted to be a part of.

What little rhythm I thought I had developed with the horse evaporated away as I went into crisis mode. I tried to pull the horse back with the reins, but to no avail. I dug my feet in to its side, but that only seemed to make it go faster. As Simon and his horse sailed over the jump, followed by the other residents on their horses, I had the distinct feeling that at any moment my life would flash before my eyes. As the jump approached at break neck speed (I now felt I understood where that expression came from) I made one last desperate attempt to stop the marauding beast. I let go of the reins and raised myself from my seat and grabbed the vehicle around the neck with both arms and whispered in its ear something along the lines of, "Wo haaarrgh, staaaaaaap,eeeeeeagh, ooooo." It worked! I nearly fell off, but it worked! Somehow I had managed to communicate to my friend that I was indeed a mere human, and as such, I was there to be intimidated by the sheer magnificence of my mentor. It did, however, obey the directive of creation and come under submission, even if it was after a little encouragement. It seems encouragement is something all God's creatures need. The kids were happy. They thought it was great fun that the Youth Worker was less competent than themselves, at horseback riding anyway.

I learned a couple of good lessons too. Firstly, don't ride a horse, even if you're paid to do so! Secondly, and more importantly, I learned it was okay to let the kids see my weakness and vulnerability. In fact, it was beneficial to developing worthwhile relationships with those particular residents. They realized they were better than me at something, and that seemed to open doors of communication, which were closed before. It seemed I was not only the helper, but I was also someone who needed help, too. And not only that, I was someone with a sore bottom who needed help! All very funny, but making for a great time together. As we completed our time, we decided to dismount (guess who thought of that one) and walk the horses up the hill. The light-hearted banter seemed to cease as our conversation relaxed into reality mode.

I began to see Simon very differently. Yes, he was only fourteen, but he had a more mature head on his shoulders. He had a certain maturity when talking about horses, which now began to flow over into other areas of conversation. In confidence, he spoke to me of his abused background. He had not been able to live at home for many years. He did not tell me all the details, but it was clear his father was the problem. How badly he was affected, I did not know, but here and now, he seemed like any normal fourteen-year-old having fun and chatting with friends.

Over the next few weeks, we became friends, well sort of. I did not really see much of him, but when I was at Hebron, he would seem to want my company and friendship. By the time he left the shelter, I would not have considered us close, but we did have a mutual respect and genuine type of friendship.

The next time I heard from him he was in prison. He called to let me know he was being released from prison in a few days and asked if I could help him. He was many miles away in another city at the time, so I was unable to visit him, but I said I would be there to help him should he return to Brisbane. He was very pleased about that and said he would see me in the next few weeks. He never turned up.

The next time I heard about him, I was left shocked and dazed. He had broken into a house, and stolen, amongst other things, a hand gun. He had then proceeded to assault a woman and take her hostage. After much negotiation with the police, he shot the hostage and then himself. I was only told the story second-hand, so did not know many of the details. My friend, who related the story to me, told me the negotiating police officer told him he had never heard such a horrific story of abuse as Simon had told him.

He seemed such a great kid, with a real love for life, and now he was gone. Oh yes, it was unjustifiable what he did in his last few hours, but maybe without the abuse he had received, he may have turned out a little differently.

For all his errors, I still have fond memories of him and wonder what life could have been like for him if he'd had a decent, loving father.

CHAPTER 5

Sally & Norman

Set a guard over my mouth, LORD; keep watch over the door of my lips. (Psalm 141:3 NIV)

DUE TO THE FACT that they could only stay for a maximum of four weeks, there was a constant turnover of residents. The average stay was three days. In the past, when I had been a volunteer, the maximum stay was only up to three days. I guess that was good for the emergency situations, but not good in giving time to find longer term solutions for residents.

We saw between two-hundred and fifty to three-hundred residents each year. This led to the dynamic for a part-time worker to turn up for work with a house full of totally different residents than the last time they worked. This would happen for me quite often, which made each shift at Hebron a learning curve, as the group dynamics of the house were always changing. One of my great learning lessons was through a brother and sister, Norman and Sally.

As I arrived for work wondering who and what to expect, I walked into the house to be instantly confronted with Norman's beaming smile. He gave me immediate attention as if he was meeting an old friend, and not a total stranger. I felt uneasy with this, as it usually meant there were underlying emotional needs which would rise up when least expected. He was tall and slim, with short blond hair and rosy complexion. As we chatted, I discovered he was sixteen years old and staying in the shelter with his sister. Whatever subject we talked about he had a comment, though his comments did usually show how very little he knew about the subject. He came across as very hungry for attention. He tended to invade my personal space and it was somewhat uncomfortable for me. His sister, Sally, came out of the girl's bedroom and sat in the living room area. Norman took me over to introduce me to her.

Sally was extremely different, to say the least. She didn't seem to want to know me or give me the time of day. They seemed like day and night in their personalities. She was short and seemingly overweight. Her long brown hair fell over her shoulders and looked grubby and unkempt. She looked scruffy in her baggy oversized clothes. Her most striking feature was her eyes. Well, not her actual eyes, but the "bags" under them. They were the worst case of bags under the eyes of anyone I had ever seen. It was hard for me to look away from them, but I knew I must, or risk the possibility of alienating her even more against me than she seemed to be already. My heart went out to her. She looked, in every way, the saddest, sorriest case to look at I had ever seen in Hebron. It was a shame she made staying with us difficult for herself. She was not easy to get along with, in fact, she was quite hostile. Even my simplest attempts at conversation were treated with contempt and anger. I soon discovered the reason for her bag problem, drugs. Sally was addicted to prescription drugs, and as I was to discover, had no intention of giving them up, not yet anyway.

As I inspected the boy's bedroom, I discovered Norman seemed to have an addiction also, a most unusual one, toys! It seems he would spend all his money on toys. This seemed unusual, as most of the guys his age I knew usually bought knives, cigarettes, soft drinks, or candy, but never had I seen any buy toys. He liked to talk about them and play with them. He was very affectionate towards his toys.

Since I had been working at the shelter for a while, I found myself in the dangerous position of thinking I had residents all figured out. I reckoned I could spot what the kids problems were a mile away, and not only that, but I knew the answers to their problems as well. Of course, I hadn't come to this conclusion without good reason. It's pretty obvious to any intelligent minded adult that if a child has problems being able to look after their money, you teach them how save and spend wisely, and then their financial problems will be gone. The same with drugs. Get them off the drugs and everything will be okay. Unfortunately, life is not always that simple. Fortunately though, God is good.

I discovered, in the case of Norman and Sally, that there is a fine line between gaining insight into a person's problems, and judging the person. It always seemed easier to lay blame for a resident's life on the resident themselves. After all, they were responsible for their own decisions which led them being in the shelter. Or were they? It was beginning to seem all too easy to tell them to get their act together and expect them to perform better. I suppose it's like parents who lecture away at their kids, thinking their talking is really getting through to them, when in fact it is often pushing them away.

I had answers in mind for Norman and Sally which were very comfortable answers for all their needs. Comfortable answers are fine I suppose, if you are a Youth Worker trying to get the job done as quickly as possible. Comfortable answers are not always real solutions to problems though. I suppose a lot of the time, I only had the residents themselves to work with and I knew if they did nothing about their position, no one else would. Some kids did change from time to time after times of counsel. Many didn't.

As a Christian, I firmly believed that if the kids committed their lives to Jesus, then everything would work out fine for them. This idea, too, over time, in my idealistic thinking, was to prove something of a disappointment and challenge for me. (More on that in a later chapter)

Sally & Norman

Though my faith would grow stronger as God dealt with my preconceived ideas, the ways in which I learned to adjust my thinking were not always pleasant. Inevitably, God taught me about myself and life around me through the lives of the kids I worked with. They contributed to my life in such a special way, and yet they probably never even knew it. Did I help them as much as they helped me? I'm not so sure. My brief involvement in the lives of Sally and Norman was a chance for me to learn.

Now, as I saw it, I obviously knew the answer to their problems. It was simple. Get Sally off the drugs and she would be fine. Give Norman support to organize and spend his money more wisely on sensible things, and he would be fine, too. Fortunately for me, and even more fortunately for Norman and Sally, I never had the chance to give them the "wisdom" of my counsel. Alec called me into the office to give me the low-down on Norman and Sally's situation.

They were staying at the shelter while their family situation was being assessed by the Department of Family Services. This involved themselves and their parents being interviewed and assessed to see if the family home was a suitable and safe place for them to live. A happy story had not emerged.

It was no wonder the both of them had problems. In fact, any normal person having to go through what they went through would have had any number of physical, emotional and mental problems as well. Sally and Norman's addictions had very little, if anything, to do with personal logical choices; they were victims of child abuse.

Child abuse comes in many forms, and at various levels, all of which are insidious. Sally and Norman's abuse had been primarily sexual. I don't desire to go into the details of their abuse; suffice it to say that it was sexual and their parents were the instigators. Who in their right mind wouldn't want to take drugs after such humiliating and degrading experiences? It sure made buying toys, as a source of comfort, seem a pretty fair option. Who was I to come along and lay my guilt trips on them? They had enough to work through. The depth of their trauma would be something I could never understand. I don't know how long it would take for them to overcome it. Could they ever fully overcome it?

If I'd had the chance to share my shallow and empty words it would have been an embarrassment. But I learned a great lesson; sometimes all we can offer is love.

Love can be made to seem such an insignificant offer at times, and yet many of the kids I knew, were crying out for love. Many could never remember receiving any. Love in action was what they needed, not empty words. Yes, professional help, long term care and stability and, hopefully, getting to know Jesus one day were things they needed. But practical love that listens, accepts, cares, and supports, goes such a long way in helping to bring comfort and relief.

In the case of Sally and Norman, I learned not to assume that a resident's behaviour could be readily explained and fixed by my simple assessments, and even more simplistic answers. The residents, like all of us, were complex people. Their problems were complex, and the answers to their problems were even more complex! It's so easy to look at our youth and say they just need a kick in the seat of the pants or to go out and get a job. Many have deep and far-reaching issues that few people would want to think about, let alone have answers for.

CHAPTER 6

Life & Death

My soul is weary with sorrow; strengthen me according to your word. (Psalm 119:28 NIV)

PROBABLY ONE OF THE most disappointing lessons I had to learn was that when a resident became a Christian, it did not always guarantee a happy life, free from the effects of sin. This truth came home to me in a way I would much rather forget.

Sarah was one of the bitterest children I had ever met. Bitterness seethed out of her. As soon as she arrived at the shelter, there were constant problems between her, the staff, and residents. Sarah stayed at Hebron for less than a week, but within that short space of time, she managed to alienate herself against everyone she met. Each staff worker, at the end of their shift, would be exhausted from the constant verbal abuse and endless power struggles with her. The kids were sick of her constant attention seeking and causing arguments with everyone. The headache of finding her somewhere to live was spared me as she decided to leave suddenly one night, leaving all her clothing at Hebron. I knew she would be back one day.

When I did see her again, it was in stark contrast to the girl who had run away from us. It was about four weeks later when one of the staff walked into the office and announced that Sarah had arrived and was looking for her clothing. I went straight out to meet her to sort things out. I expected trouble, as quite often when a resident departed hurriedly and left their clothing behind, other residents would take what they wanted before we managed to lock items away. The usual scenario was that the resident would eventually turn up again, demanding their clothes exactly as they had left them. This often led to quite volatile situations when we could not comply. This is what I expected with Sarah, and given her history, I expected an even worse response from her. I figured fireworks would be the order of the day, if anything was missing.

I found her on the front veranda, searching through her sports bag of clothing. As I approached, she looked up and her light brown eyes met mine in such a way as if she was trying to see right inside my soul. I must say, I was taken aback by her eyes. They had seemed so hard before and now they seemed gentle and soft. When Sarah had stayed with us, she had never given any positive eye contact. Her stares had always been the sort that made you feel you were hated and despised, and cut right through you. But now, dare I say it, there seemed to be something different about her. Her eyes revealed a change in her. Instead of the brash confidence which she usually displayed, there was a certain shyness about her.

She fumbled about in her bag and mumbled that something was missing. "Where are you staying?" I asked. She looked up at me, smiled, and said in a soft tone of voice which seemed to be looking for approval, "I've become a Christian." Before I could say anything she continued, "I've moved in with a Christian family, and it's great."

The more we spoke that afternoon, the more her countenance brightened. Not that I could take any of the credit for that, but I could tell Sarah's life had been touched and changed by God. God alone deserved the credit for the miracle I was talking to. As Sarah left, I remember thinking I had just met a young woman who had found meaning and hope. How we praised God for the transformation in her life. Little did I know, I would never see her alive again.

The magazine story had made it sound all so cold and calculating. It was obvious from what was written that the writer had few real facts at hand. It did make quite a sensational sounding story. "Teenage girl dies on streets of Melbourne from a drug overdose." That girl was Sarah. The story was written in a Christian publication and went on to ask where had all the Christians been for someone like this girl. It implied that if Christians were out doing their job, none of these sorts of things would happen. Maybe there is a challenge for Christians to get up off their chairs and become good Samaritans, but that was too late now for Sarah. And anyway, Christians had helped her, and look where she ended up.

It's much easier to understand God when things are going well, but it sure tests your faith when adversity strikes. Who really had let this girl down? Was it Hebron? Was it me? Maybe it was the family she had been living with? Could it have been God? I discovered that once you start making a list of who is at fault, that list can just go on and on. My reasoning at the time told me that ultimately, sin was the culprit. Not primarily individual sins, which do come into the picture, but rather sin as the disease that has infected all humanity.

One day, Jesus will return and sort things out once and for all. Until then, we have to battle on with the strength that God provides us. These thoughts, and others, consoled me at the time. Sarah's death was a sad loss for me. Having experienced something of her transformation, I just felt so disappointed at such a waste of life. Sarah's death brought home the fact that every life is fragile. At any time, day or night, a life can be gone. If only we could always be aware that each person is precious, and every second we spend with someone is a precious moment as well. It also brought home the fact that becoming a Christian does not guarantee an easy road ahead. I don't fully understand why Sarah ended up dead on a Melbourne street. Was it temptation? Could it have been visiting friends who suggested one last hit for old time's sake. I will never know. But I have used her death to try and encourage others. I have preached and spoken to young people in the church, pastors, youth leaders, etc. on the danger of thinking that when someone becomes a Christian, the church has finished its work. Becoming a Christian is not the end of the journey; it is the beginning of a whole new adventure. Every new Christian is a babe in Christ, needing nurture and care to be able to grow to maturity. Fostering that care is also the work of the church. Using Sarah's example, I've told people how special their life is to God and that he is always there for them. I used to think Sarah's young life was wasted, but I now realize it wasn't. It's helped others to realize the importance of salvation and discipleship. And best of all, I get to see her again in heaven.

CHAPTER 7

Changing Places

For we are God's handiwork, created in Christ Jesus to do good works, which God prepared in advance for us to do. (Ephesians 2:10 NIV)

DIRECTORS CAME AND WENT at the shelter. The general policy of Teen Challenge had been that the director was changed every twelve months due to the demanding nature of the work. Alec had now been at the shelter for nearly two years, and though exhausted, seemed to thrive on the workload. It was something of a shock when he quite casually one day, right out of the blue, offered me his job.

We were in the office checking the telephone answering machine, he turned to me as he listened to messages, "Teen Challenge has offered me another job and I'd like you to take over here." "But wouldn't that be Claude's decision?" I asked. "I've already spoken to Claude," he retorted, "and he seemed quite worried you wouldn't take the position. But I said I thought you would." Alec said, with his usual silly grin.

It would be a big decision for me. I would have to leave Bible College. I would be "on call" twenty-four hours a day, seven days a week. I would have the full responsibility of running the shelter; if anything went wrong it would be my neck on the chopping block. It was a good time to evaluate my journey with the shelter so far.

I remembered back to my original involvement. When they asked at church for volunteers at Hebron House Youth Shelter, I had little idea of what the work would involve. None the less, I had a sense from God that I should offer to help, so in faith, I thought I should step out and give assistance. The situation was that workers were very tired and they needed people to relieve their shifts, so they could have some much needed time off. I didn't fully understand what that meant, but it sure seemed there was help needed and I thought I could offer some. At that point in my life, I was having a difficult time in my own Christian walk, however, I felt very strongly that God wanted me to help others as part of my service to him.

The difficult time in my Christian walk was actually being exacerbated by the fact that I had made this decision. I had been involved with a small Christian fellowship group who had helped me greatly with my walk with Christ. I found myself surprised to find that, on discussing the volunteer work with them, they seemed against the idea. The way they saw it, I was doing the wrong thing. Their interpretation was that I was seeking to earn my salvation by trying to do good works instead of trusting in the finished work of Christ on the Cross. Their decision was extreme, to say the least. They said I was blaspheming the Holy Spirit. Needless to say, I was devastated and was in a sort of what I called, "Spiritual shock." These people were the only Christians I had been meeting with on a regular basis and it led me to be in a deep depression.

Maybe I had not really heard God? Maybe they were right? But in my heart I knew that I had heard God. I knew, too, that salvation should produce good works of some sort. I felt sure God was telling me he had blessed me, and he wanted me to a blessing to others. I knew my Christian walk still left a lot to be desired. I still smoked, partied and was generally on about my own "junk," but I knew God was calling me onward and upward and that it had to do with my serving others.

Changing Places

To become a volunteer, I had to attend an interview at Hebron House, which I stumbled through. I was asked many questions by the acting director, Helen, but on reflection, the only one I could remember was when she asked if I was a Christian. I was feeling such a failure at the time that I could not look her in the face as I answered. I just looked at the ground and mumbled, "Yes, but not a very good one." Helen was very gracious in her reply, saying, in effect, that it is not easy for anyone to be a good Christian. Interview over, I was accepted as a volunteer and would do my first shift the next Wednesday evening.

My own personal trauma aside, I was very happy to be seen as useful to someone.

Wednesday came around quickly, and before I knew it, I was parking down the side street next to the shelter. There was a back door which I could see was open, but I thought it best to go in the front door, so I made my way there. As I approached the front door, I hesitated. I stood still, staring at the open doorway. All at once the situation hit me. I was going to help others. I, with all my problems, was going to minister to the youth of Brisbane. Who was I to do such a thing? There must be better qualified people than me to do this work?

I really believed God had called me to this point, but now I found myself in a bit of a panic. What would I do? What would I say? Would the staff and residents like me? Would they see my faults and misgivings? I was still trying to come to terms with rejection from those closest to me, now I felt vulnerable again. I prayed along the following lines; "Father what am I doing here? I have no idea what to do or say. I have come to help others, but now feel I may not have what it takes. Please tell me what to do. I ask in Jesus' name, amen." Amazingly, the answer came immediately. The Holy Spirit spoke into my heart; "Acceptance. Just accept whoever you meet in there. No matter what they do. No matter what they look like. No matter what they say. Accept them in the same way I accepted you." I didn't fully understand the implications of what the Lord had said, but I did have a direction for my work. I was to accept others in the same way God had been willing to accept me, and that was unconditionally!

Five hours later, I walked down the back steps towards my car, having finished my shift. I must say I felt a little confused. I did not feel I had done very much. Had I really helped? Had I been of any use?

I was not fully sure of the answers, but I did know one thing; I had been accepting. I had sought to do what the Lord required of me, and although I had many issues running around in my mind, I knew that I had made a start in the direction the Lord had given me. In knowing that, I was content. I knew also that a tired worker had been able to have some much needed "time off" away from the pressures of the work. God had spoken to me by the Holy Spirit which began to put to death the notion that I had done what my "friends" had said and blasphemed the Holy Spirit. I had been saved to serve, and the adventure was beginning to unfold!

These thoughts, together with the fact that the Lord had previously specifically answered my prayer for a paid part-time position in a Christian organization, helped in directing me to take up Alec's offer.

To be honest, it was a job I had wanted from when I first went there as a volunteer. I had prayed for the job a number of times over a six-year period, but never had the peace of God to apply for it. Now the timing was different. I would be the next director of Hebron House Youth Shelter. Praise the Lord!

CHAPTER 8

Director's Tears

Those who sow with tears will reap with songs of joy. (Psalm 126:5 NIV)

I'M NOT SURE WHICH book it was, but I remember reading somewhere that to be a Christian leader you have to be able to cope with loneliness. I thought this was a good idea, as I had always preferred solitude and quiet rather than crowds and noise. I also felt a strong call to Christian leadership, so I thought I must be cut out for it, as being alone was no problem for me. As with most things in life, I was to discover that the harsh reality of experience can be far different from ideological expectations.

Working in a youth shelter is a stretching experience, to say the least. Needs of all descriptions confront and examine you. As director, all areas of the work fell under the umbrella of my job description. That meant anything from counseling a depressed resident, to sweeping the yard, being abused by parents, to searching for spent petty cash, attending youth sector meetings, etc. This meant that as director, I was constantly battered with requests of all types. It was as if others thought I was the one with all the answers, when in reality, from the way I saw it, I was the one with the questions many people never wanted to face.

Of all that came crossed my path, I think the hardest thing I had to do was to make terminal decisions. Terminal decisions were the ones I had to make that meant there was no going back to remake the decision. It was terminal and irreversible. Living with the consequences of a terminal decision was not easy either. These decisions often affected lives adversely, but I knew I had to make them. I alone could make the decision. It was all on me, and I alone was responsible to make the choice. It was at the point of making such decisions that I found the true meaning of the loneliness of being a leader. When there was a difficult decision to be made, which no one else but I could decide, there came a sense of isolation and loneliness which I had never experienced before.

Generally, I enjoyed decision making, as it was a skill I had acquired and worked on for a few years. That was fine when making decisions that primarily affected my own life. When I had to begin making decisions which primarily affected someone else's life that was a very different story. There was also the very real dynamic that my decisions would often be misinterpreted by others who did not fully understand all the circumstances leading to the decision and whom I was not at liberty to reveal those circumstances to. This could be very hurtful at times, but was part of the journey.

I believed I had seen some inappropriate decisions made in the past by previous directors, but I was now learning quickly that what might be viewed as a bad decision to one person could be viewed as a very good decision by someone else.

I lost a volunteer over the decision I made one evening to evict a resident. The volunteer did not agree with the decision, saying that we were there to house the kids, not to evict them. In principle, I totally agreed. In reality, I needed to evict the resident for the safety of the house. The volunteer never returned. Without detailing that particular eviction, there were many reasons that arose that required terminal decisions. What do you do with residents who throw pool balls at other residents and staff or threaten

Director's Tears

with pool cues but refuse to cease their behavior? Or the ones that use the shelter scene to deal drugs to a minor or who threaten with fear and violence? What do you do with a sexual predator? While all the cases that came through the door were needy in one way or another, there were tough decisions to be made, depending on each individual's behavior and how it affected the safety of the shelter.

The shelter had a black list book that had the names of offenders with a reason for their listing and consequences for their actions. Consequences could range from anything from an overnight ban to an indefinite ban. While I always aimed to exercise graciousness, there were cases which required strong consequences. I never really got used to having to ban someone. Often I felt I had made the right decision, but I always wondered where the person might end up, and I knew they would probably end up in a worse mess.

As far as I knew, Alec had made all the banning decisions himself, and I had just followed on with that pattern. However, I did learn to share the responsibility. Eventually, if I had to impose a ban, I would do so only up to the next staff meeting, where I would allow staff to work through with me what fair consequences should be. This gave support to my position, as well as broadened the involvement and decision-making abilities of my staff. As director, I was at the shelter a lot more than when I was a part-time worker, and the involvement in the lives of the residents was often much deeper and more varied than I had known before.

The way I managed to cope with the hardest decisions happened out of the blue one day. I had only been the director for a few weeks and I was really feeling the pressure, when this incident happened. I was in the office talking with one of my staff about the difficulties of the job, when I suddenly began to cry. It was as if the burden of the role of director suddenly hit me. All of a sudden, I saw it for the incredible responsibility it was. Right there in the office, I released my burden to the Lord. Through my tears, I spoke to him of the anguish I felt inside, the pain of rejection, the agony of responsibility, the torment of having to say no, and the wretched guilt of having somewhere to live while others had nowhere. He heard my cry. I knew Jesus understood, because as I poured out my heart, I immediately sensed his peace which passes all understanding. I was aware, too, that for him the burden was greater than it was for me. I only saw the consequences of a fraction of the resident's burdens. He saw their whole worlds.

I still had my struggles from there onwards, but my burdens were committed to the Lord who gives wisdom to those who ask, and boy, did I ask!

There would be many more hard decisions ahead but I knew there had been a breakthrough in my attitude to facing them. They would no longer just be my decisions. They would be ours, mine and God's.

CHAPTER 9

Administration & Communication

The reason I left you in Crete was that you might put in order what was left unfinished . . . (Titus 1:5 NIV)

EACH DAY AT THE shelter was tension filled. Staff were constantly overtaxed and exhausted. This was quite understandable, given the circumstances they were given to work under.

As director, I worked nine-to-five, Monday to Friday, and was on call twenty-four hours a day with the aid of a pager. In reality, this meant that I arrived well before nine and usually left after five. The pager would interrupt my sleep on many occasions, as well as many social activities. Generally, I was constantly tired and under enormous pressure, which was not helped by the fact that I was helping to run a church in my spare time.

Part-time staff were rostered on three twenty-four-hour shifts, 9 a.m. to 9 a.m., every two weeks. This may not sound like many hours, but often the staff had other jobs or studies, which needed their time and resources. The difficulty with the shelter work was the need to go home and recover adequately afterwards. It was often the case that staff were stretched to their limits by residents. They often did not gain very much sleep, and left at the end of their shift exhausted and needing time to recover. The household often came under a cloud from sheer tiredness and stress.

The demands of the residents were incessant on every level you could think of. No sooner had you answered one question there was another and another and another. One would be in tears and expect emotional support. Then another one would start some sort of attention seeking behaviour because someone else was getting all the attention that they wanted. In the midst of all this, there would be ongoing issues to deal with, some of which were minor, such as who had not made their bed. Some were not so minor, like, who had the drugs? Interjected into the general mayhem, were telephone calls, visitors, and the duties of the staff, such as driving residents to trains or buses. Add to this the responsibility of preparing meals and doing household shopping and washing, and it was obvious why staff were stressed out and tired.

Now that I was director, I was always looking for ways in which stress could be alleviated in the household. This could be in small ways, such as tying a pen to the interview form folder so that there was always a pen there when you needed one. This may not sound like much of a stress inhibitor, but it sure was better than looking for a writing implement at three in the morning when you had some Department of Family Services Child Care Officer breathing down your neck because they want to get home quickly, as often seemed the case.

I had come to realize that being well organized relieved stress. I became known as the great form inventor. (I still am by some!) By creating forms for certain areas of our work, I managed to take unnecessary stress off staff and myself. Half the work was done for us already.

An example was household shopping. We were on a very strict budget and so had to be thrifty with spending. We had our basic meals, and at times we would have treats such as pizza.

The hot bread kitchen up the street occasionally gave us bread and cakes, some of which would be frozen for later use. But we still had to shop wisely. The shopping was usually the responsibility of a particular staff worker, but due to the pressure of other responsibilities around the shelter, this was not always the case. The advantage of having a "Shopping List Form" meant anyone doing shopping, could relatively quickly assess the situation on the pantry shelves and know what to order. It may sound trivial, but it sure was effective and saved much time and money.

As in most organizations, effective communication was vital. Communication happened on various levels and in various ways. If any area of the shelter's life had poor communication, then that meant it must be worked on. This was especially so when it affected someone's life.

Each morning, there would be a handover session, where the outgoing staff would report on the previous shift to the incoming staff. This usually constituted of both a written, and a spoken report. The important thing was to pass on factual, relevant information. It was not good enough for a staff member to say what they thought might have happened, but rather report what they knew to be absolutely true. This was often crucial in the decisions we had to make. It was a waste of time to pursue an issue without relevant information or proof. If staff had reasonable grounds for suspicion, then that needed to be explained in a manner that showed reasonable grounds to pursue the matter further.

I had inherited the practice of a written report, but felt it needed to be improved upon. The reports were usually written on single sheets of paper and only lasted for a shift then were thrown away, this was a waste as far as I was concerned. Firstly, because incoming staff would only have a report of the previous twenty-four hours to make some, at times, very important decisions. I felt this wasn't always suitable as the resident could have been in the house for up to four weeks. Secondly, because it provided for no long-term record of a resident's relationship with the shelter. Such information could be valuable for the cases of those residents who would use the shelter a number of times. Thirdly, because it was a blatant waste of paper.

So with the aim of helping to improve the system, I introduced the Handover Book.

This book was simply a hardcover notebook that would contain each day's relevant information, and when full, it would be filed for future reference. There was basic information such as day, date, staff worker, volunteer, and the duration of the shift. As basic as it seemed, this information was invaluable. In the life of the shelter, a week was like an eternity, and to be able to know who was on when and with whom, was often important. As director, I could look over the pages of the book and sometimes see that certain staff or residents had a pattern of not getting along. Or it could be, that specific issues always seemed to occur with a certain volunteer. If a staff member had been on vacation, they could sit down and read through the past week or two and get a picture of what had been happening. The overall behaviour of residents was much easier to reflect on when looking at their daily journey over a period of time. It was just basic information, usually consisting of some idea of their individual behaviour and moods, as well as how the particular group was getting along, as a household. This was especially helpful for spotting mood and behaviour change in specific residents.

Any conscientious worker could come on duty and look over the past week or so and see how a particular resident was being affected. If the resident was being negative or anti-social on their shift, staff could read and maybe see that the person had been fun loving up to that day, and then start working towards identifying the problem and aim to proceed to a possible solution.

Staff could also identify any behaviour patterns that were being addressed on other shifts, and this gave an ongoing accountability for residents and staff.

The book also included any petty cash spent on the shift, as well as any outings the house had undertaken. This helped me to monitor what our meagre finances were being spent on, and who was spending it. It helped me to make sure the staff were making provision for outings, and not just leaving the kids in the house all the time. At one point, it helped me see that one staff member was

Administration & Communication

spending most of the available money for outings on their shift, which was the day after we received our allowance. I could point out to them what they were doing, and how it affected others. We also listed any disciplinary measures that were to be enforced, so it was clear to both staff and residents. For example, a resident may be banned from playing pool for a day as a consequence for something they had done. Gone were the days when a resident could play one staff off against another or escape a consequence for their actions because of a change of staff.

The Handover Book was a success, and staff were better informed. The outcome was that they felt more in control of their circumstances. The benefit for me was that they were not paging me every two minutes on my time away from the shelter.

To support the Handover Book, I also introduced the White Board. This was just a simple white board divided into the seven days of the week. Any important appointments the residents had were put on the board for all to see. There was no longer any excuse for missing a job interview or a doctor's appointment. As soon as staff began their shift, all they had to do was read the board and organize accordingly. The beauty of this for me was that staff could easily see what was required and no longer needed me to tell them all that was happening. This led to staff feeling a sense of ownership and independence in their work, but at the same time kept them accountable. So the staff now had a Handover Book, and White Board, to help keep them informed, on track, and in control.

The next item I revamped was the Interview Form. We used this for admissions, and though it was working suitably, I knew it could be improved. Along with the usual information such as age, name, etc., we added more family information and relevant key relationships. This was all done by a system of line charts and named circles called Ecomaps and Genograms. They cut down on lots of writing, but gave a simple graphic example of the resident's situation. Arriving at their shift, it could take a staff member a lot of time to read a page or two about each resident's life situation. The images worked so well that, within minutes, staff had a good overall view of each resident's situation. Again, the emphasis was on passing on relevant information as simply as possible, for the benefit of staff and residents. The Handover Book and Interview Forms particularly worked together well in the long term, also. Because the records were kept and filed away, they could be called upon and referred to when necessary.

In order to make the saved Hanover Books and Interview Forms work well, another book was introduced into the system. This listed the name of every resident and the dates on which they had stayed in the past. This was helpful as it meant that the information regarding a client could be quickly retrieved when required. This was especially helpful when dealing with regular clients and their child care workers from the Department of Family Services. Often residents and the shelter would be "set up" by a Child Care Officer. Most Child Care Officers were very good; however, some made life difficult for us.

A typical scenario was for a Child Care Officer to place a child in the shelter and say they would move them by a certain date, only to leave us exasperated when the day would arrive and the Officer would be on vacation, or away at some staff development day, or unavailable due to it being their day off. Apart from being annoying for us, I thought it was irresponsible of the department. Sometimes, you may not hear from a particular Child Care Officer for a number of months, and then when you did, it would be in the middle of the night when staff would have been woken suddenly by the telephone, and be required to make a quick decision.

But due to our new system, whenever anyone asked for a placement, my staff could look up the files and gain relevant information on which to base their decisions. Imagine the response of a Child Care Officer at 2:00 a.m., being greeted with the fact that months ago they dumped a kid on us and did not follow through with their side of the bargain. It may not have changed the decision we had to make for the sake of the resident, but often it allowed us to call the officer to some commitment between us before, giving them our answer. It also let them know that we were organized and prepared to challenge their role in dealing with the shelter.

Administration & Communication

Overall, the reality was that being well organized made life easier for staff. It gave the shelter an edge and sharpness and a reputation of being on top of the job. When there was a need, as things arose, other modifications to procedures were addressed. The main thing was to have a system of effective communication, which helped take some stress off of the staff, while, at the same time, improving the service to the residents. After all, they were why we were there. There was, however, one communication innovation the residents loved to hate, the chores list.

One of the biggest areas of argument was the question of who did which chore and when. It may seem like a trivial issue, but when you are a tired and stressed out worker, you have better things to do than waste time debating who did which chore, when. The chore list made it easy. Each time someone was on a chore, such as washing up or clearing the table, their name was entered on the list at the appropriate place. When it was time for new chores to be issued, any complaining along the lines of, "I always get that chore," or "Staff always give them the better jobs," could very easily be settled by pointing to the list which featured chore activity over the past few days. Argument over, peace restored, more important things to get on with! Why there had never been one in the past, I never knew.

Having forms, and such things as a Handover Book, may have seemed like unnecessary red tape to some, but when used appropriately, it improved service supply, relieved staff of needless stress, and allowed the shelter to run a little more smoothly than it had done before.

Being organized not only made sense, it helped set us free to focus on the important work, the lives of the residents.

CHAPTER 10

Angie

> For you created my inmost being: you knit me together in my mother's womb. (Psalm 139:13 NIV)

My introduction to Angie was not at all like any of my other first meetings with a prospective resident. It was quite by accident that I walked past the dining room door and caught a glimpse of someone at the bottom of the stairs. That someone was Angie. She was not alone. There, in her arms, was a young man. I was to discover this was not unusual for Angie. From where I was standing, it seemed that their tongues were so far down each other's throat, they would require surgery to separate them, much as Siamese twins do. I was just about to make my presence known, when the guy extracted his tongue, said a swift farewell, and disappeared down the driveway. Angie just kept watching him until he was out of sight. Without raising her head, Angie picked up the small sports bag by her feet and proceeded up the stairs.

She was short, medium build, with blond shoulder length hair, which was in ringlets. Still in her school uniform, of a white blouse with pleated knee-length navy blue skirt, white ankle socks and black shoes, she looked quite innocent but I guessed she wasn't.

Angie

Judging by the kiss I had just seen, I thought this fourteen-year-old girl was not as sweet and innocent as her appearance suggested. Not that I wanted to prejudge her, I just wanted to keep my mind open to options. I knew Angie was fourteen, because I had been alerted to her upcoming arrival. Her boyfriend had telephoned earlier with some bizarre story of a girl with no home to go to, as home was just a prison from which she had to escape.

He was playing the part of a Good Samaritan and doing his best to help her. I discovered he even paid for her hair to be styled to help disguise her. Her life was described as consistently going to school and returning home to be locked up and isolated from any chance of going out and enjoying herself.

As Angie approached the top of the stairs, she raised her head and our eyes met. Her eyes were pale blue and conveyed anger. I smiled and said, "Hello." She looked at me and said, "Hi," as her head turned away, only for her to glance back at me as if to check out if my smile was genuine or not. As we chatted in the office, she seemed quite blasé about her whole situation. Apparently, Angie was fed up with being at home and so Angie was leaving. It was as simple as that to her.

She would manage to survive, or so she thought. She would find part-time work, stay with friends or find her own place. To her, everything would be simple and straight-forward. Angie knew just what she wanted and where she was going, but sadly she only had assumptions of how she was going to get there. This was not unusual for someone in Angie's position.

Most of the runaways that came through the shelter, usually had some major problem at home. They stayed at home as long as they could stand it, but the day would eventually come when they thought they were big enough to fend for themselves in the big wide world. And so they would leave home. Angie was a typical example.

Sitting in the office speaking through her bitterness, the story unfolded of a very spoilt adoptee whose limits were being restricted by some very strict parenting. Locking Angie in her bedroom at night in an effort to control her, was not a great way for her mother to show she cared. Angie was almost seething as she related the story to me. The lack of trust and the manner of dealing with an emerging adolescent had led to a total breakdown in the parent and child relationship.

It was obvious from the contemptuous way Angie spoke to even me, a total stranger, that she would not be an easy person to live with. But, it was the same sad story of a parent trying to bring up a child of the twentieth century with nineteenth century methods. And here was the result, a bitter and hurting individual wanting to escape the genuine care of a mother, which regretfully, had been displayed inappropriately. But life was not going to be as simple as Angie wished it to be.

First, I told her I had to call her mother and let her know Angie was all right and where she was staying. Angie didn't like this idea, but it sounded a better alternative to her than that of calling the police to see if she was listed as a missing person. She was quite adamant about keeping the police out of the equation. I thought that was fair enough; they have enough criminals to deal with, without getting bogged down in family disagreements. I telephoned her mother, who seemed more interested in chewing my ear about all the bad things Angie had done, rather than being happy her daughter was safe. Angie had a few words with her mom, which were very hostile even over the telephone, and I shuddered to think how they must relate face to face. Mom wanted Angie home and behaving herself. Angie would only go home if she was given more freedom to do her own thing. They had a stalemate. Not unusual in this type of situation. Neither party was prepared to negotiate, unless they could have their own way. They would not agree to sit down with a third party to work it through, so I ended up giving Angie a bed for the night to give them some time to think about what they were doing. Though it was her first time in a youth shelter, Angie quickly made herself at home, too much so in fact. She quickly became a ring-leader.

Angie was excessively manipulative and with dashes of cunning and malice together with an obviously high intelligence, made herself the queen of the castle. Her attitude toward staff was

Angie

quite brash in an almost snobby sort of way. It was as if she knew she was better than anyone else and so proceeded to act that way. Of course I did not learn this just in one night. Angie stayed on for a while. Angie and her mother would not get together, and so Angie was still determined to go it alone, however the shelter had a responsibility as she was only fourteen years old. Due to her age and the possibility of being put in moral danger as a minor, Angie's situation had to be brought to the attention of the Department of Family Services. The Department would be able to offer some monetary assistance, as well as work closely with the family, and hopefully bring some kind of reconciliation to all concerned.

The reconciliation never eventuated. Angie's lack of co-operation saw to that. After a year or so of seeing Angie in the system, she was just one miserable child who was sick of the system, with no permanent home, and quickly running out of patience. Angie was in and out of the shelter at various times.

Over the month's Angie and I became friends of sorts. She was still a free spirit, but at least there was a mutual respect and a sense of a working friendship between us. In my work with Angie, I'd always tried to be fair and consistent, and I think she had learned to respect and trust me. The last time I saw her was the day I left on vacation. I said, "See ya later," to all the kids as I usually did, but totally by surprise, Angie rushed up to me and threw her arms around me. She gave me one almighty hug. I don't recall any previous physical contact with her, as that would have been inappropriate, so this was a shock to me.

Weeks later, when I returned from vacation, Angie was gone. But it sounded quite positive. She had gone to live in a family situation and had returned to school, and was going to complete her senior year. A few weeks later I received a letter from her which confirmed Angie was still with the family, and trying hard at school. I was pleased she had written, as it affirmed she was really trying to succeed. I wrote and encouraged her to continue the path she was on.

This was quite amazing, really, as the Angie I knew had never been so stable and positive about life. I really thought her life was going to work out fine. The last news I heard of her was disheartening. Angie had left the family she was with and left school, and had gone table top dancing and was possibly involved in prostitution. She was sixteen.

I could never work out why her life took that course, but I may have found a clue a few weeks later. I was cleaning out the security cabinet in the office when I came across a grubby piece of paper which was folded to the size of a business card. It had obviously been carried around for a while by someone, as it was pretty scruffy on the outside with dog-eared corners. As I unfolded the paper; I had no idea of the profound effect it would have on me. It simply said;

> Father 17 yrs., Height, Five foot six inches, medium build, likes surfing.
>
> Mother 16 yrs., Height, five foot two inches, slim build, likes the beach.

It was from the registry office and belonged to Angie. It was a description of her real parents.

I was deeply saddened to realize that Angie must have carried this around with her, and now she no longer had it and I had no way of contacting her. I know it was not much, but I'm sure to her, it meant a lot. I believe it helped me understand her a little better. Having grown up without a father, I know something of what it is like to search for your identity. I knew what it was like being an adolescent, needing a father's guidance and having none. Angie had seemed so restless so much of the time. No amount of money offered by her adoptive parent could entice her to change, or bring her peace. Even when offered her own hairdressing salon to secure her future, Angie turned it down. Money can be helpful, but it does not meet the deep emotional needs. I wondered now if Angie was searching for the deep need of just simply knowing her real family and finding her true identity. I can imagine her searching questions. What did Mom and Dad look like? What did their voices sound like? Do I look more like Mom or more like Dad? What would it feel like to be held by them? Do I have siblings?

ANGIE

Then there would be the more difficult questions to face. Why didn't they want me? Did they love me? Was I a mistake? Should I never have been born? Are they alive? Will I ever see them? Such questions can bring a life of emotional and mental turmoil. It can be difficult for people who have come from a loving, functional family and home life, to even consider the sense of loss in someone who has never known their real parents or family. Reading Angie's grubby piece of paper, made me realize, yet again, that each resident's life was a learning curve for me. No two were ever the same.

I have a lingering sad personal footnote when it comes to Angie. At the time Angie was at the shelter, my wife and I were involved in a community program supporting local families. We would take in a local teenager who was having problems at home and they would stay with us for an open period of time so things could be worked on with the family by the Department of Children's Services. Though Angie did not live in our area, we were asked to consider taking her into our home. After due deliberation and prayer, I said no. It was the right decision at the time. But some days I just wonder if . . .

CHAPTER 11

Liar Liar

What a person desires is unfailing love; better to be poor than a liar.
(Proverbs 19:22)

LIARS MAKE HONEST PEOPLE doubt the truth!

Please read the above line again. Liars making honest people doubt the truth was a real revelation for me. This came through a specific incident when the shelter was broken into. Given that locks only keep out honest people, it was not unusual to find the shelter broken into at times. It was rare that we left the shelter unattended, but at times it happened. Often residents would arrive home early from wherever they had been and become bored with waiting for staff to arrive, so as any normally bored person would do (I jest), they would attempt to, or actually succeed, in breaking into the house.

On the occasion in question, I had been out for the day and left the house unattended and arrived back at the shelter in my car. As I drove into the driveway, the back door of the shelter was open and there with his head sticking out of the door was Justin. He looked straight at me with a look of horror, closed the door, and disappeared into the house. By the time I entered the house, there was no one in there and the only clue to any intruder was the open window which had probably been used as the way to get in, as well as his escape hatch. But I had clearly seen Justin.

Justin was staying at the shelter, and he seemed a genuine sort of kid with a difficult family background and a penchant for stealing anything that was not bolted down. His blatant exposure at the rear door meant a stern talking to would be required, with an understanding that it would not happen again. Nothing was missing, and it seemed more like a boyish prank to show-off to the other kids.

A short while later, Justin arrived home with a big grin on his face when he saw the other kids, but which quickly changed to a deadpan expression when he saw me looking at him. I asked him into the office where we both made ourselves comfortable, me in an armchair and he on the sofa. I did approach the situation a little tongue in cheek, as I had caught him at the door; he had seen me and was well aware I had seen him. I simply explained that he had been caught and that an explanation was in order. I thought it a mere formality from there on in. How wrong I was. He said he was never in the house!

I could not believe what I was hearing. I explained I had seen him. He just remained silent and looked at the floor. I thought a few minutes would be all it would take to gain a full confession, but no, he stuck to his story. Now, in some circumstances, I may give someone the benefit of the doubt, which invariably I often did as I did not really see my role as that of a detective. However, in this case I knew I had seen the offence take place with my own eyes and there was no way I was going to pretend that the incident had not happened. I continued to seek a confession but it was not forthcoming.

Time was ticking away, and we had been in the office about an hour with still no satisfactory resolution in sight. I was starting to get pretty annoyed with Justin and could not believe he could tell such a barefaced lie without even so much of a change in his demeanour.

As we talked of the incident, he just told lie after lie, I was quite amazed, this guy was not just a good liar (if there could ever be such a thing) this guy was a great liar. I reckoned he really believed himself.

His insistent lying then had a profound effect on me. I could hardly believe it, but I began to consider I may have been wrong. The mere thought of this was preposterous. I had seen him clearly, at close range, there was no mistake, and yet here I found myself, doubting what I had seen. I felt very strange. It was then that I realised that liars make honest people doubt the truth.

I left him in the office by himself and went for a brief walk. I went over everything in my mind again and affirmed to myself what I had seen. It felt unusual to doubt when I knew I had no doubt.

By now three hours had passed and as I entered the office once more I decided to take a sterner attitude. I explained there was no doubt in my mind as to what had happened and that even though there was no confession forthcoming there would be a consequence for his actions. If he did not admit to what happened, then he would be expected to find somewhere else to stay.

I did not expect it to come to this, but the house had been broken into and there was some minor damages and if he was allowed to get away with it with no consequence, then he would not have the opportunity of learning that his behavior was unacceptable. I had decided not to have the expectation that he would be aware of himself and experience guilt for his actions, as I wasn't sure he thought he had done anything wrong. The way I saw it, as long as he got away with it everything was all right. The crime was not the issue, getting caught was.

I met this attitude often, but here was an extreme example of "not owning one's behavior." Most kids told lies to cover up their offences, but usually after a period, the confession would come as the guilt of their crime took hold. Justin appeared to feel nothing. and seemed quite convinced of his innocence. But now, for Justin, the tide was beginning to change. He knew from the little time he had been around me that I was true to my word. If I said he would have to find somewhere else to stay, then he knew he would have to find somewhere else to stay.

"I did it," he said, without as much as a flinch. I was dumbfounded. I just stared at him not knowing what to say. This guy had wasted nearly four hours of my time and now when it was to his advantage and he had something to gain, he owned up. Now I really felt like throwing him out!

I asked him to explain what happened, and he did. He explained every precise detail, including the reasons why and how. It had all been to show the residents how skilfully he could break into the shelter. As he spoke, he was fighting to hold back the smirk which wanted to take complete control of his face. I was not impressed. Justin was allowed to stay, because I did not intend to become a liar and go back on my word. However, he did leave for fresh pastures the next day.

I had learned an important lesson. No matter how much I knew to be true, if someone lied, then the truth could be doubted. From thereon out, I sought afresh to identify the obvious lies of residents and reveal them, not for the case of a power struggle, but so they would hopefully learn that lies do not serve them, but that they could become the slaves of the lies they tell.

All staff and volunteers were required to avoid lying for any reason. There was nothing to be gained if we used a lie to manipulate or control the residents, or to make life easier. Liars eventually got found out. There was a worker at the shelter who would tell incoming enquiries that the shelter was full and that we could not take in anymore kids. Over a period of time, it was revealed the person had been doing this to make their shift easier. The lie was discovered. Apart from the fact that you can't hide anything from God, you also have to have a very good memory to be able tell a lie without being found out. Often, with the residents, all I had to do was ask the same question a number of times and their different answers revealed they were telling a lie of some sort.

Lies were not a good foundation for the residents to build their life on. Some of our most effective work in a resident's life was done after we had managed to cut through all the lies that camouflaged their life. A new foundation of honesty and truth helped build trust and openness, and a way forward. Often it was in baby steps, but they were still moving forward.

CHAPTER 12

The Sting

> Hide me from the conspiracy of the wicked,
> from the plots of evildoers. (Psalm 64:2 NIV)

SECURITY WAS ALWAYS A problem at the shelter. There was the obvious need for the material possessions of the shelter to be secure. We also had to do our best to make residents feel they were in a secure and safe environment. As director, I also had the safety of my staff and myself to consider.

Because we often had petty criminals staying with us, we soon discovered that if we did not bolt something down, it would eventually go missing. I quickly learned that our facility was not impregnable. In fact, it seemed just the opposite. If someone wanted to break in, then they would simply break in. As we had learned from the example of Justin, there really seemed no way to stop them. I think Alec had once told me that locks only keep out honest people. He was right. We did, however, discover ways to deter would-be thieves and others who would try to enter the house without our knowing. It was indeed a slow process, as it was usually only after someone had broken in that we worked out what to do, or took the necessary steps, to prevent it happening again.

After each break-in I would gain insight as to how the criminal had actually done it. I had to think like a criminal. Honest people don't think that way. It was a challenging learning curve.

For instance, there was the mystery of the unforced entries under the house. The shelter was an old Queenslander style house, and was built on stilts and therefore, had room underneath for storage. We divided the downstairs into sections that had specific functions. One section had the washing machine and sinks, and was available for the residents to do their laundry and for staff to do the household chores. Another area had craft tools and equipment for doing leatherwork, and would be used from time to time as an activity center for the residents. There was an area full of clothing for any residents who required extra clothes. We also stored all our sporting and gardening equipment, as well as tools and odds and ends under the house.

Now, our problem was that though the downstairs door was padlocked, uninvited guests somehow still managed to work their way in there. We could find no sign of forced entry and were quite frustrated by the number of times the offence took place. The main frustrations were, that when someone broke in the downstairs section, they inevitably created a mess by searching for clothing and just throwing what they didn't want on the floor. They often stole sporting equipment and wrecked the craft section, for no reason at all. This led to staff requiring time to clean and tidy up and put things in order again. Time was the one thing staff never had enough of, so this regular occurrence was a frustrating concern. Often, we felt that the residents knew what was happening, but there was no way they would run the risk of telling tales on another resident, and especially so if it was one they considered a friend.

The downstairs section was fenced around rather like a picket fence, and we figured that maybe some of these pickets were being removed to enter, and then replaced on exiting. This was a long shot but a possibility all the same. One idea we came up with to combat this possibility was to consider inserting steel reinforcing, of the type used in concreting, on the inside of the downstairs fencing. Reinforcing was purchased and bolt cutters borrowed, and within a few hours the job was done. Frustration upon frustration, they still got in! Not only that, but we had put a new lock on the large old freezer where we kept the sporting equipment, and that too had been broken into again. There was nothing else we could think of to do.

We were baffled and beaten. Then one day, quite by accident, the solution to our problem smiled sweetly upon me, or maybe it was God who smiled sweetly upon me. I just happened to walk into the dining area, and out of the corner of my eye I spotted movement through the open rear door. A resident was just stepping off the back door steps and heading for the downstairs gate. I nearly called out to them to say if they needed something from under the house they would need the key to get in, and a staff member to be with them. Due to the problems we had been having, the downstairs was kept constantly locked and was out of bounds to residents unless accompanied by a staff member. Almost instinctively, I sensed I should keep quiet and just watch. I figured I may learn something. And I did.

Hiding myself partly behind the doorframe so as not to be seen, I peered down the stairs watching the resident fumbling around with the pad bolt and padlock, which secured the door to under the house. In a few moments, the door was open, and the resident walked in under the house. I didn't waste a second, but ran down the stairs quickly in order to see just what had happened. Had the locked been picked? Did they have a spare key? On close inspection, and much to my surprise, the padlock was still in place on the catch, but the bolt had been freed to enable the door to open. I called for the assistance of the door opener.

The solution was so simple I could have kicked myself for not having seen it before. The steel clasp on the padlock, when moved into the correct position, was not thick enough to prevent the arm of the bolt from passing over it and so the bolt could be slid to the side without unlocking the padlock. A simple manoeuvre, but not knowing this had it given us some pain and grief over the months. Once a new padlock, with a thicker clasp, was in place the unwanted entries downstairs ceased.

Living a Sheltered Life

Time and time again I learnt of ways to break into houses simply through the different ways the shelter was broken into. It's surprising how easy it is to remove sliding glass doors and windows. Who would have thought to lift roofing iron and enter in through the ceiling trapdoor? The simple ways to manipulate locks and catches without leaving a trace of evidence. I even learned how to break into my own car without having to break anything at all, and only using a hair comb.

We became quite high tech by installing movement detectors which were nicknamed, A.F.D's. meaning Anti Fraternization Devices. This was employed on the night shift after all residents and staff had retired to bed for the evening. The operation of these units was quite simple. Should anyone move through the living room, pool room or kitchen during the night, then a small alarm would go off in the staff bedroom. As boys will be boys and girls will be girls, this alarm system received plenty of use. One of the humorous aspects of this was that residents, after they had been at the shelter for a while, understood what the function of the A.F.D's. were, and did their very best to beat the system we had setup. I'm sure some of them thought staff must never sleep, as they were constantly caught whilst on evening manoeuvres. There was probably no funnier sight than catching a resident on all fours moving like a sloth, trying to defeat the device, but they never did. Of course the A.F.D's had the broader function of being a burglar alarm when the house was, at times, left empty, but it was as a night time sentinel that they got the most use. Inevitably, we realized that if someone really wanted to break in, they could not be stopped, all we could do was to protect and defend our castle as best we could.

A past resident did break in and took our video player and boom box. He turned up later with his parents and Child Care Officer and apologized. But we never got the items back.

Of course, there was not just the threat of the residence being broken into that was of concern. There were thefts in the house that happened periodically. My worst experience was what I personally referred to as, "The Sting."

THE STING

They got me hook, line and sinker! I could not believe it. They had played me. Sitting at the lunch table, the kids were so well behaved and talkative. As a couple of the kids asked to leave the table, I never suspected that a setup was on. Mark and Jenny had left the table and were chatting in the living room. Ian sat on my right-hand side, which meant when I spoke to him, I was looking away from where Mark and Jenny were. The office door was open, as usual, because I was always going back and forth throughout the house. Ian seemed to particularly want to talk to me, which was somewhat unusual for him, but was quite normal in that residents often became talkative after gaining a sense of security and friendship with staff.

If I turned my head towards Mark or Jenny, Ian would say or do something to grab my attention. In particular, he was very merry and laughing. If it had not been for lack of symptoms in his eyes, I would have been sure he was taking the travel sick pills the kids used to get high on. The main point was, he was keeping my attention.

There were two doorways into the office, one on my side of the house and one on Mark's side. Unbeknownst to me Mark had sneaked into the office while Ian acted as a decoy, or was it Jenny? I never suspected a thing until later in the day when I went to get some petty cash out of the cabinet, and there was none there. The cash box had been forced open and all the money taken, $50 was gone. Our weekly budget was only $170 per week for food, gasoline, entertainment, etc., so $50 was a large sum to lose.

I did not need to be Sherlock Holmes to work out what had happened, but I was very hurt and held a deep sense of betrayal. Here I was trying to help these kids and they do this to me. Biting the hand that fed them was not clever at all. Still, they were survivors and did what they felt they needed to do. Some of them had little or no income, so stealing was a way of life for them on the streets. But this was not the streets, stealing from the shelter that was trying it's best to help them was not a wise move.

What really surprised me was their stupidity. How could they think they would not be found out? Who else could have done it?

Of course, the usual lying took place to justify actions and point the blame to others. As no individual culprit would come forward, I knew justice needed to be swift. Once Child Care Officers had been consulted and last chances had been given, I dealt out the consequences. Mark went to another shelter, and Jenny and Ian were allowed to stay but were grounded for the remainder of their time.

There had to be some consequences for their actions, so in a way you could say, in the end, I had the last laugh. Perhaps, but I did miss the fifty dollars. Mark had ended up at another youth shelter and a worker there said he was bragging about the $50 he stole from Hebron House. His Child Care Worker was informed that he would not be allowed back at Hebron until the $50 was repaid.

The Sting, and many other incidences, eventually led to us purchasing a combination safe big enough to house the petty cash tin and any important documents. Because anything of real value was in the safe, even if residents broke into the office, they could not steal anything of worth.

Still, locks indeed, only keep out honest people.

CHAPTER 13

Public Relations

Listen, for I have trustworthy things to say;
I open my lips to speak what is right. (Proverbs 8:6 NIV)

ONE OF THE ROLES the director had to fulfil was that of spokesperson at speaking engagements, and to a steady flow of visitors. Public relations, I think they call it.

Visitors came from various backgrounds and for various reasons. There was always so much work to be done at the shelter, that I would avoid spending time with visitors or at speaking engagements, if I believed it may not be productive in some way. I personally considered my time as one of the most valuable assets I had, and I never enjoyed wasting it. However, public relations was part of the job, so it had to be done and, at times, it was very worthwhile.

There were the usual meetings with representatives from the government to ensure we were not misusing our funding. Inevitably, excuses would be given by them as to the reasons why more finance could not be made available.

Politicians would frequent Hebron, usually around election time. With their entourage of TV and media personal there would be pictures of handshakes for the newspaper or videos made for the TV News. We had to protect residents and make sure their images were not recorded for public viewing. If a comment was used from a resident their name could not be used in any news media.

Numerous community groups would come to visit or invite me to speak at one of their meetings. I enjoyed the chance to speak at community meetings when I knew it could be worthwhile, because it gave me the opportunity to speak openly and honestly about the plight of our homeless youth. This was a very eye opening experience for many people and I always felt that if people understood better what was happening, then they were on the way to hopefully doing something productive about it.

My talks very often centered on a similar theme. It seemed to me that the problem of homeless youth was not one that was going to go away, and was in fact, a consequence of a very real social problem, that of family breakdown. It may all be very well for people to talk about freedom and the rights of the individual, but what about a thought for those who are affected by such freedom of choice. More often than not, in a family situation, it was my experience that the children bore many of the consequences of their parents' decisions.

Countless times, I heard the story of the child who was in the shelter because mom or dad had remarried and the new partner did not want a child from a previous relationship in the house.

Often, it was the scenario of a parent who no longer wanted their child around, as they didn't want them to discourage any possible future relationship with a potential partner. This was brought home to me with one incident, when on an evening's outing, the staff took the household to a Blue Light Disco run by the police department. There, on the dance floor, was a lady bopping away who was recognized as being a mother of one of the children staying with us. When approached with the fact that her child was present, the parent responded by saying, "I don't want anything to do with her, she cramps my style." It may seem hard to believe, but some parents have little or no natural affection for their children.

Public Relations

Then there were the parents who did not want their children at home because of their inability to control the child's behavior. But where did the child learn most of that behavior in the first place? My guess was, most likely, in the family home. Parents go for many years failing to provide adequate discipline for their children, and then want to just walk away from the situation and expect someone else to pick up the pieces. There are always consequences for actions.

At many of the places I spoke, the general assumption was that these kids on the streets were needing a swift kick in the pants and sent home to get on with a normal life, like the rest of us. I must say it does sound a good idea, but in reality it does not always work so simplistically. I remember a staff worker returning to the shelter after dropping a resident back to the security of a house and family. The worker was shocked at the conditions she found at the family home. There was human excrement in many areas of the house, there was rubbish everywhere and the stench was such that the worker almost vomited on the spot. So much for sending kids home where they belonged.

I also spoke of other serious issues that would prevent children from returning home; such things as various forms of child abuse, lack of financial resources, inadequate housing facilities and constant family conflict, which had never been resolved. One fifteen-year-old girl told the story of how every time she did something wrong, her mother always said to her, "I knew you would never be any good ever since that day you sat on my spectacles." (Which had happened when the girl was aged eight!) The harsh truth is that most unresolved family conflict was more serious than just sitting on a pair of specs, and could have been going on much longer than seven years.

Then there were the parents who would come for some family counseling, which on the surface seemed to be a good thing but quite often ended with no resolution at all. This was not because there wasn't the opportunity for things to be sorted out, but because the parents generally came with the attitude that it was the child who needed sorting out. Do that, and everything will be fine was their attitude. Forgetting, of course, that they may have some part to play in the way their child has turned out, and maybe there needs to be some changes made in their own lives in order to help the family win through to a satisfactory solution. But sadly, many parents could not see that they had any real part to play in the way their child had turned out, and so, felt the problem was with the child, and nothing to do with themselves. I spent many hours with traumatized parents in deep anguish over the plight of their child, but it was rare for me to find one who was prepared to change their lifestyle for the benefit of that child.

I never purposefully set out to a speaking engagement with the intention to shock people, but I did aim to speak honestly and openly and aim to give clear insight into some real issues behind youth homelessness. The main challenge I gave to people that were considering looking at ways to help homeless youth, was to consider to becoming a volunteer with an organization working in the field.

Indeed, there may not have been enough money floating around and more financial support could be helpful if used wisely, but what the kids really needed was genuine care and concern. Kids needed to know, in practical ways, that there was someone there who cared enough to spend time with them.

Actually, we all need that.

CHAPTER 14

Prayer

..., pray continually, (1 Thessalonians 5:17 NIV)

THE SHELTER WAS NOT a place to enter without prayer. Whatever the combination of residents and whatever the group dynamics were, there was always room for prayer. Prayer made a difference.

At the commencement of each shift, there would be the handover time. This involved the outgoing staff sitting down with the incoming staff and furnishing a report on the previous shift. This report involved some details of each resident's behavior, and some information on the group dynamics. Each handover time began and concluded with prayer.

As the shelter was a busy place, time was always of the essence and invariably the handover times were too lengthy, as staff needed to go home. This, however, was not the main concern. While the handover time was in progress, the residents were left alone to their own devices, which was not always a pretty sight. Apart from the obvious squabbles between residents, there would be the occurrence of such things as food being stolen or chores not being done and worse still, residents taking off for the day before there was time to interview them.

It was a frustration, but it was necessary for all staff to be involved in the meetings for the benefit of keeping the day rolling and being well informed. The benefits of the handover time outweighed the deficits. We believed, and experienced, that prayer changed things. Each resident was prayed for each day, either generally or specifically, as well as praying for whatever was planned for the day. If ever the day lacked prayer, the worst of days would be had.

There was an incident one day when the whole household of residents seemed to be going crazy, to the point where they were even climbing up on the pool table. No amount of reasoning could change their behavior. Needless to say, the situation was dangerous, and becoming more dangerous by the minute. There were two staff, Barbara and myself. Even the motherly figure of Barbara couldn't get through to the kids.

Barbara was usually in control and generally had the respect of the residents, because of her fairness in decision making and her warm and loving attitude. Barbara was the mother figure that the residents could confide in, if they chose to, and they often did. The residents treated her with respect, and because of that, Barbara usually had the house running in good order. But this day was different.

I had just arrived back to the shelter from a meeting at head office, and had walked into this inferno of youth emotion and antics. I could not recognize any of the usual physical symptoms to confirm my suspicions, but it was almost as if the residents were all spaced out on drugs. That was the way they were acting, hysterical laughter, abusive language, threatening behavior, but they didn't look drugged. I tried to help Barbara settle things down, but it seemed as if we were just not there. The residents would look at us, but take no notice and make no response. It was as if we were transparent and they were seeing right through us. We decided to pray.

Barbara and I went into the office and closed the door to the surrounding mayhem. We just handed the situation over to God, in the name of Jesus Christ. That's basically all we did. We were not sure what to pray for and just asked the Lord to take control. We then walked back into the expected smouldering cauldron. To our amazement, the cauldron had stopped boiling. The residents had settled down and were acting and talking as if nothing had happened. As far as Barbara and I were concerned, it was a miracle, a practical example of the power of prayer.

This was not just an isolated incident. There were many other times when all that seemed to work was prayer. I felt it was one of my chief roles to make sure each day was adequately prayed for and that my staff practiced the art of praying for each day's work and for the residents and staff. Hence, the importance of a prayer time in the handover meeting. The emphasis was often on prayer with action.

Job hunting for a resident would involve our praying for them. They did not always know this, but we would commit them to the Lord and ask him to guide their paths. But as well as prayer, we would at times, support the job hunt with finances or a lift in the van or whatever we could do to help them succeed. Prayer was backed up by actions; we did not just expect every answer to prayer to fall out of the sky with no action from ourselves (though it sometimes did). We had to put ourselves in a position for the prayer to be answered. For me, the prayer life of the shelter became a testimony and encouragement that God was with us.

We did not rely on coincidences. We relied on God-incidences.

CHAPTER 15

Daily Dangers

... and why do we endanger ourselves every hour? (1 Corinthians 15:30 NIV)

To some, working in a youth shelter might seem a romantic notion. Some see it as being on the front line of Christian mission with people who really need you. Others see it as being able to help those less fortunate than yourself in a really practical and relevant way. Still others, see the chance of having the opportunity to share your faith with someone who would rarely have the chance to hear the gospel message. It all may seem such a wonderful life and calling, and indeed it is, but it is not a life I would encourage people to enter into lightly.

I entered into the shelter simply because I knew they needed volunteers and I felt God giving me the nudge to respond. I had no formal training, and had absolutely no idea what life was like in a youth shelter. I hadn't a clue how the residents would respond to me, and as it turned out, I had even less of a clue on how I would respond to them. In fact, I only had one thing in my favor, the sense that God wanted me there. The call of God proved to be the critical element in my youth shelter experience.

Daily Dangers

I discovered that the shelter could be, and often was, a place fraught with danger, and for me, was no place to be without a strong sense of God's direction. This is not to label those youth who enter shelters as all having the same faults. But, every now and again, the shelter would find itself in situations which were extremely volatile and dangerous, and often for no apparent reason.

Consider the mix: a teenager between the age of 13 and 17, experiencing trauma of some sort, thrown together with up to (sometimes more) seven other traumatized teenage strangers, and a grownup or two, whom they have never seen before in their life, who is suddenly telling them what they can and cannot do. The potential for disaster is quite understandable, under those circumstances.

As a worker in the shelter, one of the main priorities was to see that residents and staff were safe. All arrivals were asked to hand over any weapons they had with them. Generally, this led to knives being handed over, and an array of martial art weapons. Sometimes, the word would get around that there was a knife loose in the house. We usually found the hiding place, thanks to an informant. But, probably, some of the most dangerous weapons were those that belonged to the household. The pool table was a great place of contact with the kids, but no place to be when the pool cue was being used for a weapon, not to mention the times when staff and residents had to avoid low flying pool balls because someone decided they wanted to take their frustrations out on someone else.

Then there were the times when a fire would be lit close to the house and, even occasionally, under the house. I can only say it was by the grace of God that the virtually all wood constructed house never totally went up in flames.

One day, a volunteer came to me and said that one of the residents was cooking something, even though he had been told he was not allowed to at that particular time. I confronted him at the time, only to be responded to with the threat of a pan of hot fat thrown at me. As the person making the threat grabbed the pan of hot fat from the stove as they spoke, I considered it a genuine danger.

Then there were the times when relatives would visit and be unhappy with the situation and decided for themselves that it must be the fault of the staff that their kin was living in such a place. So, of course, the obvious thing to do would be to threaten staff, who were the easy targets to vent their anger and frustration on.

Past residents would sometimes return to pick up items left behind, and then end up not wanting to leave because they have seen a friend there, or spotted someone they fancy. Getting them out of the house was the easy part (sometimes), but then they would just go and stand at the bus-stop across the road and never board a bus. Their hanging around all day, or all night in some circumstances, would often be a constant temptation for residents and a major hassle to staff. If the past resident was unhappy for some reason, then threats to staff or residents would usually ensue, often nothing sounding too serious, but just enough to have to keep an eye on the situation and make sure residents didn't get into a fight with the perpetrator, or worse still, abscond with them.

Drugs could always be a problem, both legal and illegal drugs. Some residents who came to stay, actively promoted drug use to residents behind the backs of the staff. The environment was such that street hardened kids would be living with just your average kid next door, and the street kids wanted to reinforce their perspective by trying to lead others down their pathway of life. Drugs was one way to do this. To combat this, all medication or drugs of any description, had to be handed in on arrival. Medication was handed out by staff, as needed, and residents were observed to see if any were showing symptoms or drug use. This was simply done at times when residents were relating to us in ways that seemed different from their normal interactions. This might include such things as excessive giggling, vomiting, dilated eye pupils, or maybe just a spaced out look. The hard part was that cheap, legal drugs could be purchased from the local pharmacy and consumed before arriving home to the shelter and take effect sometime later. It was difficult, at times, to control, but fortunately, not every resident who came through the door was into drugs. Some were into sniffing gasoline. Usually, this meant the lawnmower and fuel had

Daily Dangers

to be locked away, as you could bet your bottom dollar, if it was not, someone would try to sniff it. The same was true of other substances found around the home that could be sniffed or taken to promote some sort of a high. Everyday items had to be locked away to prevent the occasional resident from seriously damaging their health.

Alcohol was a banned substance in the house, and any residents who arrived home drunk were to be told that there would be no bed for them that night. This did not really work in reality, but it was a deterrent for some, but many was the time we had to deal with the consequences of alcohol abuse.

There was also the danger of sexually active residents. Apart from the obvious danger of disease, there were those whose only aim, it seemed, was to get in the sack with the most innocent, inexperienced partner they could find. Of course, sex was out of bounds in the shelter, and we even had an alarm system fitted so that staff would be warned if there were any night-time prowling going on. I did not want the job of telling any irate mom or dad that their little rose petal had gone and got themselves pregnant while in my care, and fortunately I never had to.

As well as looking after their physical safety, we would also seek to care for their mental safety. Videos were not to be too violent, and our rule was generally to select PG rated ones. Television was allowed, but again, shows that were too violent were not encouraged, and we aimed to view mainly family type shows. Music was closely monitored, and though a broad range of music would be allowed, we steered away from lyrics promoting or encouraging violence, suicide or death themes, and sexual promiscuity. As the residents thrived on their music, we aimed to keep it as positive as we could to promote healthy attitudes and not destructive ones.

There were already plenty of negatives in the lives that came before us. As staff, we wanted the shelter to be a place of hope and not one of despair. We felt there was already enough of that in the kids' lives. That is why we tried to make the shelter look and feel like a home.

We believed that if the shelter was kept in good appearance and state of repair, it helped with the idea that the residents were worth something to us; they were important. The fact that we aimed to provide a pleasant environment said this to them in ways in which words could not.

The residents respected this approach. They saw the shelter as their home while they were there, and generally looked after the place. After all, it was there for them and needed to be there for others who followed them.

A pleasant home environment also offered some sense of emotional security and nurture through difficult times, which was all part of our offering protection from dangers.

The shelter was indeed a place of many dangers on many levels. It was not a place for the faint-hearted or the glory seeker. It was a place where the call of God was paramount to being an effective worker. The attitude and gifts provided by God were the foundation of being an effective worker. A staff member had to be constantly aware of the situation in hand, and have a calm head and heart to handle any situation that arose. Protection and safety of staff and residents was the first priority, and this could be better guaranteed by having a positive structure in place with relevant and effective guidelines and procedures. Yes, at times it seemed legalistic, but in the majority of situations there was much grace found in times of need.

Working in the shelter could be seen as something of a romantic notion. It was amazing how many volunteers changed that notion after just one shift.

CHAPTER 16

Make 'em Laugh

...Do not grieve, for the joy of the LORD is your strength. (Nehemiah 8:10 NIV)

THOUGH LIFE AT HEBRON contained much sadness and anxiety, all was not miserable. There were times of much laughter throughout the house. In fact, humor was a very important prerequisite I looked for when interviewing potential staff. I figured life was tough enough on the kids without having to be looked after by a miserable, stone faced youth worker.

When a child was at the shelter, it was usually at a very traumatic point in their life. But even in the midst of life's traumas, I always felt there was often something that I, or a member of staff, could do to put a smile on a kid's face.

Most of the time, we all enjoyed sharing stories and laughing together. However, there were times when laughing at a resident's story was not appropriate. The residents would tell these stories seriously and with such conviction, but you would not want to crack so much as a faint smile at what they would tell you, for fear of offending them. You would know they were either exaggerating or lying, but at times, they just needed someone to listen. Often it

Living a Sheltered Life

was a sign of how boring and meaningless life seemed for them. They had to make up stories to make their life seem interesting. Some stories I would hear were pure fantasy.

One such a story was the sixteen-year-old who said he could hit a one cent coin dead center with a Kung-Fu throwing star. That may not sound too difficult to do, but when he went on to tell me he had achieved the feat by throwing the star 800 meters (approximately half a mile), I must confess I doubted him.

Then there was Terry. Even his crimes would make you laugh! While staying at the shelter, Terry had supposedly gone to look for a job, but what he actually found was a police cell. Terry had been walking around the local shops, when he suddenly decided he needed some money. Out came his pocketknife as he walked into a florist's shop and demanded money. Not wishing to oblige, the florist refused to part with any money. Terry accepted the refusal and walked out of the shop. The proprietor duly called the police. Where was Terry found by the police? Sitting just feet away from the shop, playing with his knife in the gutter, next to a police car! Just knowing that Terry would try such a stunt was a joke in itself. The fact that he was sitting next to the police car somewhat summed up Terry's expertise at crimes. If it hadn't been such a serious offence in the eye of the law, I'm sure I would have laughed longer and harder.

Then there was the self-titled, "Mick 'EEL' Dundee". This lad was too young to look for a job, and for the time being, no school wanted him. Each day, he would go down to the nearby creek and search out eels. At first I thought it sounded quite dangerous, until I saw the monsters! He came home with a jar full of the creatures one day. The biggest was the size of a round shoelace but only about six inches long. The fact that they were all transparent made the smaller ones pretty hard to see at all. He made us all laugh with his daily antics. The sheer joy on his face as he showed his catch was worth a million dollars. He had a zest for life, which sadly, many of the kids who came to the shelter seemed to have lost, or at least forgotten about for a while.

Make 'em Laugh

It wasn't just the residents who gave us plenty of laughs; the staff had their fair share of humorous experiences. Like the time Brad woke in the middle of the night to find someone out on the street standing on our trash can, taking the road signs off their posts. As someone who had considered becoming a police officer, Brad dutifully telephoned the police and then proceeded to go around to the front of the house to await their arrival. To his utter and complete surprise, the police were already there. While taken aback at the swift response of the police, Brad walked over to them to explain what he had seen. As Brad approached the police, he noticed flashing lights coming down the street in the direction of the removed street signs. To his astonishment and considerable embarrassment, there was a semi-trailer carrying a house heading towards him. In effect, Brad had telephoned the police to report someone removing street signs, who were in fact house removers working with a police escort! No harm was done, but it did make for a real laugh at the handover meeting the next morning.

At times, the kids were observers of the frailties of the staff and had many a laugh at their expense. One of the funniest incidents they told me about was the time when one of the staff marched out onto the deck area to lay down the law to the kids. The story goes that the worker marched out of the office, through the games room, slid open the large glass sliding door leading to the deck, and began to scold the kids regarding the noise they were making. The worker then spun round on their heel, and proceeded to walk back into the house. The only trouble being that they walked, not through the open side of the sliding glass door, but straight into the door itself! But the part that really made the kids laugh was that the worker just bounced off the door, gave it an indignant look, and walked through the open doorway into the house. This particular worker did not like the kids having a laugh at their expense, which made it all very funny for the kids, and as no one was really hurt, I must say I found it doubly amusing.

There was also humor in the little life moments that happened with residents. Barry taught me not to judge by outward appearances, and it happened in a cute and amusing way. In counseling terms they call it, Object Language, implying that the objects people wear say a lot about the person they are.

From head to toe, Barry sure looked a mean creature when he first arrived. He walked up the back steps, straight into the house, and dropped his bag on the floor. I was standing there quite speechless, just staring at him. He noticed my entrancement with a wry smile, which he tried to hide. I think I had given him the type of response he was looking for. His feet were shod with big boots to which chains had been attached, for effect. His grungy looking, black jeans were tucked into his boots, whilst held around his waist with a black, multi-studded belt. Looped around his waist, suspended through his belt straps, were more chains. More chains were to be found on the blue denim jacket he was wearing, as well as a further collection of studs. Various occult symbolism was roughly painted on the back of the jacket. Underneath the jacket, he wore what, at first, appeared to be a plain black tee shirt. Later, when he removed the jacket, I discovered it had a grotesque picture of a skeleton face on the back. All this was topped off with a skinhead haircut, and a number of holes pierced in his left ear with a collection of various ear-rings.

I introduced myself to him and led him to the office to be interviewed. On first appearance, I did not think he would last two minutes in our company. He looked a walking menace, and I immediately considered him a threat to the staff, kids and the house in general. As I interviewed Barry, he appeared quite a nice guy though on the inside, but he was trying to act very tough by giving me the impression he really didn't want to cooperate. I was not sure he would settle into the household, and thought it best if a close eye was kept on him. We went out to the kitchen where I introduced him to Barbara. Barbara, a Youth Worker, was a lovely lady with a grown up family and most of the kids who came to the shelter called her "mom". Amazingly enough, within two hours after his arrival, he was washing dishes at the sink with Barbara. Washing the dishes with Barbara was not the really amazing part of what was happening. The amazing part was that as they stood side by side, Barry was resting his head on the shoulder of Barbara as they washed dishes together. "He's a real pussycat," Barbara told me later. It's no wonder the Bible teaches that God looks at the heart, not outward appearances. I had tried to judge Barry from his outward appearance, and it just doesn't always work that way. Barry turned out to be a real encouragement and support around the house, and by the time he left, we were sorry to see him go. Without a word from us, he even changed his appearance to be a little more subdued and less shocking. But my favorite memory of him is with his head leaning on Barbara's shoulder. A lovely and cute moment of significant humor for me.

Of course, there were many times of laughter on our outings. Playing sports, bush walks, picnics, etc., often led to some hilarious times of laughter and joy. At times, laughter was a great medicine and often brought a particular child to a point of trusting me or another person, and made it possible for them to share more deeply about their problems. I personally discovered that a sense of humor, wisely used, was at times like healing oil in the lives of the staff and residents. Not frivolous and unnecessary humor at the expense of a resident or staff member, but good, wholesome, down-to-earth humor that everyone could enjoy. Humor, when under control and used wisely, is a great reliever of stress and tension. Many times I had to use humor as a type of pressure relief valve. When dealing with tense situations in the day to day running of the shelter, humor was a veritable asset. I considered the ability to use a sense of humor wisely as a tremendous and important gift for any of my staff to have. Even better if they laughed at my jokes!

CHAPTER 17

Faithful Volunteers

...my co-workers for the kingdom of God,
and they have proved a comfort to me. (Colossians 4:11 NIV)

THE SHELTER WOULD NOT have been able to stay open if it had not been for faithful volunteers. Staff were usually on the brink of burnout most of the time, and a good volunteer would be a real asset and worth their weight in gold.

Volunteers were just ordinary people, and as such, came in all shapes, sizes and personalities. As director, I always felt new volunteers needed to be patiently encouraged and given something practical to do. As I had started life in the shelter as a volunteer, I was sensitive to the situations a volunteer may face. It was not necessarily an easy position to be in.

Staff were often so busy that volunteers had to fend for themselves. This was not too bad when volunteers had gained some experience, but could be dangerous for a new one. It was not easy to train volunteers, due to the circumstances which included; limited volunteer time on the job, staff too busy with residents to have time for volunteers, and limited training materials.

The one plus was that the only real way to learn the job was by doing the job. As I saw many times over with students from various training courses, no amount of classroom learning ever took the place of being able to handle the work where it really counted, in the shelter under war conditions!

Knowledge, expectations, etc., were of little value if a volunteer couldn't use common sense and apply some practical diplomacy. In effect, the shelter itself sorted volunteers out.

Those who came for the glory soon discovered the only way to get it was by hard work and the blessing of God. They didn't hang around long. (Any glory was for God anyway.)

Others didn't like the hard decisions that sometimes had to be made. These were usually for the safety of staff, residents, and volunteers! Tough love we called it. They never came back.

All the volunteers who came in were sincere, well-meaning people, with a lot to offer, but not all of them were cut out for the work. So, a short involvement was natural and normal for many of them. But there were those who hung around.

What made a good volunteer? I'm not really sure. Each volunteer was an individual, and as such, brought something different to the work. An individual's personal talent, or gifting, was important for some. People would say to me, "How do you do such work? I could never do anything like that." To me, it seemed natural and normal, and I could not understand why everyone wasn't doing it. But that was my personal gifting, being outworked. I can't understand why anyone would want to be an accountant or a dentist or a road worker (I tried the latter once and didn't make the grade!). It just seems to come down to different people having different gifts.

Gifting aside, it also seemed important to me that people gave something a go. When I first approached the shelter on my very first shift, I had no idea of the concept of gifting. I was only going because I knew they needed volunteers desperately. I distinctly remember approaching the shelter and pausing outside the front door and praying, "Lord, what am I going to do here? What have I to offer the kids?" The answer came back immediately and became the backbone of all my future ministry. "Accept them," said the Lord. "No matter where they are at, no matter what they say, accept them." That was my introduction to youth work with troubled teenagers, and I have discovered since then, that it works for all types of people and ministry.

Some volunteers were slow starters; others were eager to make their mark. A new volunteer of mine, whom I had never met, turned up for their first shift and just sat on the couch and read magazines! I was too busy to instruct them in the ways of the shelter, and if I gave the person a job to do, they would do it, and then sit down with a magazine, regardless of what was going on around them.

Another volunteer just walked in and took complete control of the mealtime, organized the kids' involvement, and left me free to get on with important office duties.

Yet another volunteer would want to spend more time with me than the kids, just wanting to talk about spiritual matters and the things of God, or asking how to get a job like mine. At times it was like having an extra resident.

The worst volunteers, though well meaning, were the ones who thought they could run the youth shelter single handed. I would go into the office to answer the telephone, only to return to the scene of some major drama (sometimes the drama came to me while still on the telephone) because the volunteer wanted to exercise their newfound authority. Not recommended!!! A whole night could be spent sorting out and recovering from the action of a well-meaning volunteer (this also happened with staff sometimes) just because they wanted to exercise power, without first properly understanding a resident and household dynamics, and the perspective of staff.

One of my first rules with volunteers was not to allow them any final decision-making rights. This was left to me or paid staff. But as volunteers gained more experience, they were given greater freedom to make decisions.

Volunteers brought many wonderful gifts into the shelter, which benefited residents and staff alike. Some would bring their musical talents and sing songs and play instruments. Some would do gardening and handy work around the place. Others, just by their sheer personality, would brighten up the place.

Volunteers would range in age from late teens to retirement age. This was quite beneficial at different times. To some residents, the volunteers became a sort of brother or sister or mom and dad, or even a grandmother or grandfather figure. Singles, couples, parents, grandparents, doctors, students, home mothers, bible college students, etc. The diversity of age groups and various roles in society was worthwhile, as the residents became exposed to a wider selection of society than just the shelter staff.

The important thing with volunteers was that they were teachable and flexible. If they were not willing to learn, then they usually did not last very long. If they were not flexible, then they found it very difficult to "roll with the punches" with what life in a shelter could throw at them.

Generally, volunteers accounted well for themselves and were invaluable to the service. Many went on to become part-time staff workers, and some, such as myself and Brad became the director.

So despite all the ups and downs, dangers and dramas, traumas and problems created by inexperienced volunteers, they were the lifeblood of the agency, and the breeding ground for the shelters future staff, and I thanked God for every one of them, eventually.

CHAPTER 18

Whinge & Gripe

> Plans fail for lack of counsel,
> but with many advisers they succeed. (Proverbs 15:22 NIV)

TENSION! TENSION! TENSION! COMPLAINTS! Complaints! Complaints! The house was always full of tension and complaints! Tension and complaints from residents with other residents. Tension and complaints between staff and residents. The bottom line issue seemed to be "us and them." Us and them, residents against staff, a never ending power struggle. It was constant and extremely draining. As director, I was at times playing piggy in the middle.

Residents knew that I ran the place and had the final say on important decisions pertaining to their stay at the shelter. They knew they had to try to keep me on their side, as much as possible. Because I had been a volunteer, staff youth worker, and now the director, I had a unique insight as to how residents treated each level of worker differently. Generally, they treated volunteers almost as if they were not there. Often, instead of asking a volunteer for help, they would go directly to staff. If I was around, they would bypass staff and come to me. I would point them to staff or the volunteer.

Whinge & Gripe

The problem was, kids would try to play games to get staff off their backs. In practice, that meant I would come to work and kids would be complaining to me about a particular staff member and the decisions they had been making. Worse still was when residents got stressed about a staff decision and said nothing until they eventually exploded and created mayhem.

So, the everyday dramas between residents generally reconciled themselves pretty quickly. But when it came to staff, the residents were the goodies and staff were the baddies.

This attitude, and sense of division, was not good for the house. Staff wanted to foster goodwill in the house and didn't want to encourage a division with residents. Division was counterproductive to being able to come alongside the residents and really help them. After prayer and reflection, I decided that the problem was really a communication breakdown.

The way the kids saw it, staff were the ones with the power and the kids were powerless. This was evident with staff having the power to make decisions over the lives of the residents, and they just had to accept staff choices. It was not quite as black and white as that, but it seemed to me that was the way the residents were seeing it. Staff could spend many days agonizing over a particular decision for a resident's life, and having made the best decision possible with the options available, were left with very little space to manoeuvre. The residents did not always realize all the elements that went into making decisions for them. Even when residents were part of the decision-making process, it seemed the only decisions they liked were the ones they wanted. This, of course, could not always be possible.

I decided to take a risk and make myself and the staff vulnerable by introducing an open forum meeting into the daily program. Each day we would now have a "whinge and gripe" session (in Australia the word "whinge" means to complain over something trivial). I did not know if this would work, but in principle the idea was to let the staff and residents sit down together and be totally free to air their personal views without any form of retribution for doing so. I realized it could be threatening for all parties involved.

I was not sure if staff would take to the idea, and even less sure that the residents would. But, it could be a useful way to let off steam. I knew I had the skills to lead such a meeting, and I thought that was important for a successful outcome.

My concern was that there would be just another power struggle and it could all blow up in my face. However, the possibility could be that better communication could ensue and that the house would have less tension in it. I believed the risk was worth it. Eventually, we may not have to have a whinge and gripe session every day, but initially I thought daily was the way to go.

I had been toying with the idea for a while and wanted to introduce it when I thought it could potentially make a significant impact. The day came when I thought I would give it a try, as the house was feeling the most tension it had for a while. The particular mix of residents was dynamite, to say the least, and the whole house, residents, volunteers, and staff had been feeling the strain for a few days. I chose a time when no volunteers were on duty.

I switched the telephone over to the answer machine, assembled the kids in the living room and sat down together with them and Brad, the Youth Worker. I explained the nature of the meeting and asked if there were any whinges or gripes they wanted to share. The silence was deafening!

None the less, I continued, explaining that from where I was standing there seemed to be a lot of tension in the house and that I could not understand why. The silence continued. Not being one to give up, I began to explain how important it was that the staff know how the residents were feeling and vice versa, so that we could help each other. More silence. I was beginning to think that my idea would not work, but I knew deep down it would, if I could only get them to talk. I tried again.

I explained how I had important decisions to make and that by understanding their needs more clearly I would be in a better position to make decisions which could help them. Bingo! Jim jumped in. "We don't think Allan should have to leave today!"

Jim was seventeen and had been on the streets since he was fourteen, and presented himself as something of a role model and "street-father" to younger kids. It was good he was the one to speak up first, as I knew the residents would listen to him. "What do you mean?" I asked.

Angrily, Jim continued, "Well, Allan is our mate, and you have said he has to leave today and we don't think he should have to. He has nowhere to go, has no money and we want him to stay."

The other residents affirmed Jim as he spoke, by nodding in agreement. I don't know if anyone else noticed it, but as soon as Jim had said his piece and the other kids had affirmed him, it seemed as if tension was already beginning to leave the house.

With a sense of victory I said, "Well let me give my side of the story and see what you think." With all eyes eagerly fixed on me, I continued. "Allan has been here for three weeks. During that time, we have encouraged him to look for work, which he has not done. The money which he has received from unemployment benefit, which we encouraged him to save, he has frittered away. His uncle says he can go and live with him, which is a good place for him to go, but Allan does not want to go. On top of all that, the shelter if full and we are having to turn kids away who have nowhere to stay and who are in a more desperate situation than Allan." I had not betrayed any confidences as the whole household was aware of Allan's circumstances, as he would often tell people his plight in an effort to gain sympathy. The response I received was amazing.

Without actually turning their backs on their friend, the kid's response was unanimous that Allan should move on to fresh pastures. After all, he had somewhere to go, and he was taking a bed someone else needed.

The turnaround was amazing and extremely beneficial. The tension in the house seemed to have simply evaporated away, and whereas the residents had been alienated with staff, now we were chatting away with a newfound sense of being on this journey together. The whinge and gripe session, though being somewhat of a gamble, had succeeded. Allan moved to his uncle's house, the kids learned what sort of thinking went into our decisions, and the household was a much less stressful place to live.

The session became a daily habit, which led to much clearer communication between staff and residents, and many "all win" situations eventuated.

CHAPTER 19

Outings

So I commend the enjoyment of life, for there is nothing better for a person under the sun than to eat, and drink, and be glad. Then joy will accompany them in their toil all the days of the life God has given them under the sun. (Ecclesiastes 8:15 NIV)

OUTINGS WERE A NECESSITY, even though at times, they were a big chore and a lot of work. Because the shelter had a limited amount of finances, the area which usually missed out was entertainment. Outings came under that heading. It was therefore always difficult to find something interesting for the residents to do for an outing. Outings mainly happened on weekends but occasionally on week nights as well.

Most weekdays, the residents would have been out most of the day, so a night outing was not as crucial. On the weekends though, the residents and staff would often need to get out of the house, even if just to look at some fresh scenery. Often, the scenario was that the house was experiencing tension from everyone being home. To get out somewhere was a pressure relief valve for everyone.

Because of the aforementioned financial situation, outings were usually to a barbecue spot in a park or to the beach at Bribie Island. They were free, other than for gasoline and food. Occasionally, (very occasionally), an outing would be to an amusement arcade or a miniature golf park.

The secret of a good outing was keeping an eye on the kids. If they got out of control, the whole outing could be a monstrous calamity. Whenever I worked with my volunteer Kim, we had a plan of attack for outings. Since 99% of outings included the shelter's bus, whoever held the power positions in the bus generally controlled the outing. For instance, if the bus was unlocked when we announced an outing, there would be a mad rush by the residents to see who could get to the back seat first. Now, if a resident was on the back seat, it meant that staff or volunteers generally could not see what they were doing, so the number one lesson I learned was to get the back seat of the bus before the residents did!

Kim and I managed this by keeping the bus locked until we went downstairs to it, or else Kim would go down before I announced the outing and claim the back seat. It was a worthwhile tactic as it prevented a lot of the general damage of ripped seats and graffiti. Another benefit was that the residents knew there was someone watching them for the whole journey.

Oftentimes on an outing, we would insist that the residents stick with the staff and everyone walk around as a group. The aim of this was two-fold. Firstly, to avoid some petty thieving that went on if we visited shops. Secondly, to control the residents who were inclined to be antisocial. An example is, that in the past the shelter had been banned from attending a local cinema. The cinema owners had graciously allowed us to attend movies for just 10¢ per person. The banning happened when two residents were seen trying to have sexual intercourse on the floor in front of the front row of the movie theatre. Shelter staff had not kept the group together, and the incident was reported to management. Staying as a group could be a pain for both residents and workers, but could prevent unnecessary problems.

Outings

Outings in parks were good because the kids could run around and have fun, but at the same time you could keep an eye on them. This was beneficial when you could chat with one of the kids and gain some closeness with them without having to worry what was going on behind your back since you could see what the others were doing.

One of the local public swimming pools had a twenty meter (approximately 65 feet) diving board, and was a great place to go for an outing. I could spread out towels and claim a base camp, chat with kids as they sat with me or came to dry off. Though I did tend to have a mini heart attack every time I saw one of the residents jump off the diving board.

One of my most embarrassing moments on an outing, was watching the kids collecting autographs. This happened when the park across the road from the shelter held a "FREEPS" day. "FREEPS" was an acronym for Free Recreation and Entertainment for Everyone in ParkS. They were really good value, and the kids loved them. As we walked over to the park, we could hear the theme tune to the television show "Neighbours" blaring out. The good news, the Master of Ceremonies repeatedly told us, was that some cast members of the show would be arriving later by helicopter. A temporary stage had been built for the day and there were lots of entertainers performing. As each entertainment segment was completed, they would play the theme tune to "Neighbours" again. (Did they really have to?)

Eventually, the helicopter arrived, and out came some members of the cast to rapturous applause from the surprisingly sparse crowd. More theme tune continued, and the cast did their bit, and the afternoon drew to a close, nearly. Before the cast left for fresh fields, they came down off the stage to sign autographs. Did the residents like that? You bet they did! The majority of the kids we saw in the shelter were needy, and generally demanded prime attention. That's exactly what they were going to get from the cast members.

It created some really interesting dynamics. When I was a kid, I had an autograph book for people to sign. This day the cast was signing the resident's cigarette packets, scraps of wrinkled paper, as well as their arms and legs! To me it seemed quite bizarre, but the cast was really good about it, and the residents thought it was great. I did find it embarrassing though, given that I was in charge of the kids, and they were not collecting autographs the way I thought they should.

The main aim of outings was to have some recreation and fun, but that was not always the case. One Monday morning, I returned to work to find half the residents had been beaten up on an outing. They had gone into the city to a "FREEPS" in the City Botanical Garden and a couple of the boys had been eyeing some girls from a particular ethnic group. There was tension with some boyfriends of the girls, so the Youth Worker decided to take our group home. On the way back to the bus, they were literally surrounded by this ethic grouping. Our staff member was held back, and some of our boys were on the wrong end of a thumping. Fortunately, no one was seriously hurt.

Probably, the most satisfying of the outings was on a Sunday night. Church was a compulsory outing for all the household on Sunday night. Of course, we knew some residents would not like this, but we wanted to expose them to the church, and prayed that it would have a positive influence on them. Yes, they may not like it, but there were many other things in their lives which they did not like, and we knew ultimately church would not hurt them.

We allowed the residents freedom not to enter the church, which worked fine as a church member or two usually came and chatted with them while the service was going on, and most of the time they ended up in church of their own free will.

Without going into details, we went through a period that seemed to go on for months, with a resident or two giving their lives to Jesus just about every week. Monday morning staff meetings had a real rejoicing in them for a while there.

Yes, I found outings a big chore and a lot of work, but the benefits outweighed the cost when an alienated and defensive child began to trust staff and volunteers. It gave brief moments of sharing a normal life together.

Outings

So, apart from a thumping, attempted sex, calling abuse from the bus to pedestrians, graffiti, vandalism, spitting on cars from out of the bus window, and fighting in the bus, outings were fine, and another level of getting to know the kids. But boy, were they hard work!

CHAPTER 20

Choosing Staff

> Epaphras, my fellow prisoner in Christ Jesus,
> sends you greetings. And so do Mark, Aristarchus, Demas,
> and Luke, my fellow workers. (Philemon 1:23,24 NIV)

I ALWAYS FOUND IT a privilege to interview prospective staff. Sometimes it was on familiar territory, such as when considering a volunteer who had applied to come on staff. Sometimes that was fun, like the time Brad was lined up for an interview.

Brad had shown himself to be a willing and useful volunteer, with the qualities I thought the work required. The night before his interview happened to be the night Brad did his volunteer work. Brad had surprisingly, arrived at the shelter early for his shift before I had left for home. I just happened to mention that one of the front doors of the house was a problem and if he got the chance could he have a look at what could be done to fix it. There were twin doors, one of which was more or less permanently closed and the other which would occasionally open if shook by the wind. It didn't happen often, but it needed to be fixed.

Well, on my arrival the next morning it was very clear Brad had tried to make a good impression. In the doors there were nails,

Choosing Staff

screws, and even bolts hanging out all over the place. At first I thought there was no way these doors were going to open again, accidentally or otherwise. Of course they did. Brad had done a good job; it just looked a little (or rather, heaps) excessive. But it did show something of his desire to impress before the interview. I remember calling him and telling him I have some bad news, "You got the job." He seemed elated. So, Brad the volunteer got the part-time Youth Worker position, but not based on his carpentry skills.

Not all staff appointments were as easy to pick as Brad. Sometimes the interviews were with people who had never been in a shelter and with little or no experience of working with homeless youth. When interviews were with someone like this, then choosing the right person for the job was much more difficult. There were, however, certain criteria I looked for in a prospective employee.

Firstly, the person needed to be a committed Christian. This meant having a proven track record of church involvement, backed up with a personal reference from their Pastor or Minister, showing they were a responsible member of the Church. I would allow non-Christians to work as volunteers, so long as they did not violate any of our values. I only made this decision after prayer, and when I believed God was giving me that direction. I would not put a non-Christian on the payroll. They would not have lasted long if I did, because of the strong Christian influence and workings of the household. They would have been a round peg in a square hole. They would have been required to pray, attend Teen Challenge Thursday morning chapel services, and attend church when working on Sundays.

Secondly, I looked for signs of previous interest or involvement in youth work at some level, either in their church or other community organization. Some people would apply for the position just because they wanted work, whereas others applied because they genuinely wanted to reach out to youth. There is generally a vast chasm between the two approaches.

Thirdly, I looked at a person's personality. This was not always easy in a twenty or thirty-minute interview, but generally,

Living a Sheltered Life

I looked for a sense of humor as I thought this was a bottom line prerequisite. Also, when asked a question, I looked for a sharing of themselves with their answers, rather than just trying to give the answer they thought was the one I wanted to hear. I would observe their non-verbal communication to see if it backed up what they were saying. It was a waste of time telling me they loved talking to people if they couldn't look me in the eye in an interview.

Fourthly, I would look at a person's qualifications on paper. This has never been a big thing for me, but of course it was relevant to know. The areas they had sought to study revealed much about the person and their view of life. This was usually a good time to ask where they were headed in life and how the job they were applying for fit into that plan. This question usually put people on the spot, and to some degree, sorted out the chaff from the wheat.

I actually found interviewing people was a tremendous honor, and though some people were obviously not going to get the job, I felt each person required the same attention and respect in an interview. The final selection for a new worker would not be made until after prayer and discussion with other members of the interview panel.

Jamie was someone who matched all the correct criteria during his interview, and was accepted onto the team without a moment's hesitation. His first shift did make me wonder if I had made the right decision though. He must have been very nervous and wanting to impress, but it was as if in his eagerness he was not thinking straight. All through the day, the stress of the environment seemed to get to him. There were just so many things to think about in a shift at the shelter, and I think Jamie was a little overwhelmed. There was so much work to get done in so little time. Together, with new surroundings, new faces and a new boss, I felt it was all quite daunting for him. He had the good sense to make notes throughout the day. This would help him to remember some day-to-day expectations. He survived the day shift by just following me around, then came the evening.

His volunteer was late turning up, so I decided to hang around until she did. If we had a male youth worker on, we aimed to have

CHOOSING STAFF

a female volunteer and vice versa. (This was how Brad managed to find himself a wife, but that is another story.) Jamie began making the evening meal and decided he needed more items from the local shop, so he said he would run up in his car and purchase them. It was about ten minutes to six, and the kids expected tea on the table at a 6 p.m., which was our custom. But that was no problem as Jamie had a sporty little car, and he would be up to the shops and back in no time at all. Or would he?

Still, no volunteer had showed up, so I was left holding the fort with a tribe of hungry natives. Five minutes passed, and no Jamie. Ten minutes passed, still no Jamie. Twenty-five minutes passed, still no Jamie or volunteer. I was beginning to think he'd had an accident when after about forty minutes, he bounded up the rear steps into the dining area and on into the kitchen. Panting profusely, he began to explain between breaths, "Locked keys in car.... called brother....couldn't get spare keys to me.....had to run back...cars still up at the shops." He was still panting as we eventually sat down to tea.

It had been a big day for him, and he was somewhat flustered with all the demands, and this was a big embarrassment for him. But, he got through the day and went on to be a great asset, who I was eventually sorry to lose. Yes, he made mistakes and failed at times, but he learned from them and proved to me that the criteria I had set for employing staff worked. He had the qualities required for the job and with encouragement he pulled through and got the job done.

It was important to know what to look for in workers and volunteers, because at times, we had some very strange characters turn up looking for employment. Each person had to agree to a police check and there were times we discovered, through the grapevine, that pedophiles had tried to gain access to the shelter as workers (some tried as volunteers), so we had to know where we stood when talking to prospective employees. We actually had no way of doing an official police check, but I did have a contact who could do a check on people, and that was a great source for me.

Living a Sheltered Life

I always considered the most important asset I had was my staff. I saw it as an important part of my role as director to encourage them in their work and provide a chance for them to grow and develop in their work. I think, probably, the most crucial of job for me was to employ good staff. Fortunately for myself, and importantly for the residents, we did.

CHAPTER 21

Lost Child

For you created my inmost being;
you knit me together in my mother's womb (Psalm 139:13 NIV)

MIA WAS SEVENTEEN, AND it was written in the Black List Book that she should never be allowed to stay in the shelter again. It had been a couple of years since her banning, and I had nothing to do with that. But now, Mia was asking to come back and stay. Barbara had taken the call and had a good chat with her and gained a clear picture of her situation. I'd laid down some ground rules that Mia must abide by if she came and stayed. Mia agreed, so I went ahead and gave her a bed for the night. Her stay would be evaluated one day at a time, based on her behavior. I was not sure what to expect, but I guessed it wouldn't be an easy time for us. I could not have been more mistaken.

Coming in the evening, when I was not there, meant her interview form was already filled in for me to read on arrival the next day. It read like a girl who had run out of options. No wonder Mia was back with us. I'd seen her sitting in the living room when I arrived and she seemed very subdued.

Living a Sheltered Life

As I called her in to the office to be interviewed, I expected a very aggressive personality engaging in power struggles with me. Based on her history of being black listed, I felt it was a fair assumption for me to have. Nothing could have been further from the truth. She just sat on the office couch, barely lifted her head and answered all my questions with a soft, almost whisper like voice. I was intrigued.

After a few days, all I saw and heard of Mia was more of the same. In fact, every time I observed her around the house, she just looked thoughtful, almost as if she had something specific on her mind. She was always staring down at the ground or gazing up into the air. Even when she watched television, I could tell she was not really watching it. That gaze, that stare, I knew something was on her mind. As she was still with us when Barbara came back to work, I was hoping the staff "mom" might connect with her and find out something worthwhile. My hope was fulfilled.

As soon as I arrived the next morning and Barbara looked at me, I knew she had something worthwhile to tell me. Without breaking any confidences, Mia's blank stares began to make sense as Barbara unfolded her story to me.

At first it was a simple, straightforward story. Mia had gotten pregnant and had an abortion. I'd heard that type of story before, so nothing new there. The twist was that the social worker who took Mia to the doctor on the day of the abortion became angry with her. On arriving at the medical center, Mia had decided she did not want to go through with the abortion. Not only was the social worker angry with Mia, but she put emotional pressure on her to go ahead with the abortion. This consisted of telling Mia that a lot of work had been done to get her to this point and who did Mia think she was to say no at the last minute. It had cost people's time, work and money, and Mia acting like a spoiled brat was just not acceptable. After what felt like intense pressure and guilt, Mia gave in and went ahead with the abortion. Since that day, Mia had felt terrible and wished she had never given in to the social worker.

Mia also gave an answer for her blank expressions. She could not get one specific thought out of her head. She told Barbara she

Lost Child

was constantly wondering what her baby would have looked like. All day every day, her one main thought was what her baby would have looked like. From observing her from a distance, I could tell the thought consumed her. It was obvious Mia required some much-needed counseling.

In our day and age where abortion is prevalent, Mia's story brought home for me the glaring fact that abortion can leave lasting negative effects on some women. I wondered if Mia had received any counseling about the various ways it can affect individuals physically, mentally, and emotionally. I doubted there had been any post-abortion counseling. I never really felt Mia and I got along. It was enough to work through her long-term accommodation issues.

I managed to find Mia a long term living opportunity in a Teen Challenge home for girls. It was a new facility, and I was able to recommend Mia as a good candidate to succeed there. I think she was surprised that I thought well enough of her to make the recommendation. I never disliked her, but we just never had a rapport like I had with other kids. My heart went out to her because of her past and I was really pleased to see her accepted into her new home.

As long as I knew Mia, she always had that blank stare. I remember thinking one day that there was something about her I could never figure out. I was not sure what it was. I kept visualizing her blank expression, but would think that was not it. Something just bugged me that Mia was different in some way. Then one day it dawned on me. It suddenly hit me what was different about Mia. In all the time I had known her, she always had the blank stare, and I don't think I had ever seen her smile. Poor Mia.

CHAPTER 22

Stan

In everything I did, I showed you that by this kind of hard work we must help the weak ... (Acts 20:35 NIV)

MOST OF THE KIDS that came to us had every chance of making it in the future. Some support, good friends and family, a few hassles sorted out, and you knew life would turn around for them. But there were others who you knew would struggle through all of their life. Stan was one of these.

Stan was seventeen years of age and a nice kid, but slow. He thought slowly and talked slowly and gave a general impression of having some sort of mental problem. He was easily led by others, and usually became the victim in the house. He would be set up by the other kids and I found it hard to attribute real blame to him, as most of the trouble he got himself into was due to his genuinely trusting nature and vulnerability.

Stan was not able to look after himself properly. He was continually controlled by his circumstances and other people. He was a lost sheep being guided by whoever would help him. Well, maybe that was not quite correct, but he preferred to be guided by his peers rather than by adults, especially myself or my staff.

STAN

His mother cared deeply for him and was there to offer support, if he would take it. But he wouldn't. I spent many hours on the telephone with her discussing Stan's situation, but there was nothing that she could do for him apart from being there, if he turned to her.

He was into heavy metal music, which didn't seem to be good for him. He listened to it as if he were obsessed and brainwashed by it. He idolized a particular rock band, and they were all he wanted to talk about. It limited his conversation and bored just about everyone who spoke to him. It even tended to alienate him from many of his peers.

At the time he was staying at the shelter, he was on probation for petty crimes. This limited where he could live and where he could visit. His movements were restricted and he had to report to his probation officer regularly to show that he was keeping out of trouble and living at a proper address. He got on quite well with staff, as well as residents as he was viewed as generally being harmless. But I did have concerns about how he would manage to cope in the real world. His living skills left much to be desired, which meant he couldn't really look after himself. His personal hygiene was poor, and it followed that most of the time he carried an odor around. Apart from discouraging others by the smell, it would not have been good for his general health.

It seemed Stan's decision-making skills were based on what felt best at the time. He really had nothing going for him. How could he be expected to survive? Where was he going to get the skills? He had virtually no money, few, if any real friends, no job, no permanent place to live, and was pretty well without hope.

His plight was one of the great frustrations of the "system". What was really being done for kids like him? Where were the support structures? Where were the facilities to embrace and develop such a person to a position of security and community acceptance?

The only way he was going to survive in the real world would have to be through crime. How else can someone survive with no work skills, no living skills, no real worthwhile support structures, little education, as well as no inner personal resources to deal with relationship issues with family and friends?

Added to that was the pressure of no fixed abode, low income and a personality which inevitably led to being the victim in whatever circumstances he found himself. It's sometimes easy to think we have all been created equal with the same opportunities and that as long as we make the correct decisions, our lives fall into place. Stan's life was "behind the eight ball" from the beginning, and I knew there was little chance of him ever changing that position.

We managed to find a place for him at the Teen Challenge Drug Rehabilitation Center, which would provide twelve months accommodation, as well as some living skills and personal development training. Due to his involvement with alcohol and some drug experimentation, Stan qualified for the Rehabilitation Center, and he was willing to go give it a go. The only problem was his probation conditions. Stan was worried his probation officer wouldn't let him go. This proved to be no problem at all. Part of Stan's probation conditions was that he resided at Hebron House and could only move, if and when his probation officer said so. The probation officer had no problem with Stan moving into the rehab, and in fact thought it would be a good idea and a great opportunity for Stan.

In the next week or so, all was made ready, and all that was left to do was to take Stan to the Rehabilitation Center. But where was Stan? On the day of departure, Stan had departed all right, except not with us; He had gone his own way. I found out later Stan had got the idea into his head that because his probation officer said he could leave Hebron that meant he could leave and go anywhere he wanted to, of course this was not the case. Stan had now absconded and we could not find him to help him.

Over the next few weeks, we heard various stories about Stan's whereabouts from some kids that had seen him around the streets. Eventually, we found out where Stan was. He was in jail. Our worst fears had come true. Where else would you expect someone to end up when they had neither the means nor capabilities to survive in the harsh realities of life? Maybe in jail, the authorities might see the dilemma he was in, and look at some way of offering him hope and a future.

Too late. While serving his time in prison, Stan committed suicide. Words could not express the way we all felt. Another statistic? Another failure? Another victim? Whenever I remember Stan, one thing is for sure, he was created in the image of God and given the gift of life, and for reasons known only to him, he found death a better alternative. Those who commit suicide are often seen by society as being unbalanced in some way and are thought to have gone over the edge. Well they have gone over the edge, but what drove them there is complex.

I have a simplistic view of why people commit suicide. A simplistic view which I believe has far-reaching and profound implications. Firstly, when people are forced into a corner and they can see no way of escape, as illogical as it may sound, suicide becomes an option for them. Secondly, where there is no hope of a worthwhile life, suicide becomes an alternative.

Stan was born into a world in which he grew and developed to become a unique individual, stepping out to make his own way in life. In a sense, and without appropriating blame to anyone, it's as if he was set up. He did not have what he needed to survive. He just did not have the mental and emotional capacity. He had no real prospects of employment. He did not appear to have any real friends or lasting relationships outside of his mom. He had no support structures that he could fit into which suited his issues, to guide and nurture him. Yes, he made some bad decisions, but don't we all? Yes, he may have faced things in jail that freaked him out, but many people never see suicide as an answer, no matter what they go through. He had potentially lost hope. Without hope of a worthwhile future, is there any reason to continue on?

Please excuse my preaching at this point but too many of our youth take their own life. They need to find a real reason to live. They need to find hope. They need a reason to get out of bed each day. They need a reason to want to live. They need the hope of a worthwhile future. When a person sees the hope of having a future, it gives them a reason to live. Jesus offers hope, a reason to survive, a reason to live, a future. Our young people need hope.

CHAPTER 23

Prayer Ending

I urge, then, first of all, that petitions, prayers, intercession and thanksgiving be made for all people- (1Tim 2:1 NIV)

I STOOD AT THE rear door and watched Brad pull out of the driveway with the van loaded with residents. I closed and locked all house doors. I put the telephone onto the answer machine and made myself a cup of tea, and eased into one of the easy chairs in the office. Well this was it, my last day at the shelter.

Brad would be away for a while, in fact, I would be gone by the time he returned, and when he did return, he would be the new director of Hebron House, and I would be gone.

I wanted to be alone with God in my last moments at the shelter. Prayer was my main objective, but first I would have a time of reflection. So many faces came to mind, there was no way I could remember them all, but many I knew I would never forget. I would remember a single name and images, thoughts, and feelings would spring to mind. Some good, some not so good, some tragic, but all at this time seemed precious. It was special to sit and reminisce, and ponder the privilege of having been allowed to serve God and the homeless youth this way. I felt humbled that God had used me in such a way, and began my prayer time by telling him so.

I had worked at the shelter, first as a volunteer, then as a part-time worker, and finally as the longest serving director, and the awesomeness of my journey had suddenly struck me. I continued on in prayer with thanksgiving. I had been involved in so many lives and made so many decisions. Now, I committed each life and each decision to God for his will to be done.

I prayed for Brad and his future leadership, that God would protect him, give him wisdom for the work, and use him to take the shelter onto its next stage of growth.

Finally, I prayed for myself that I would be able to let go and get on with life without trying to hold on to the past. It had been an all-consuming work, especially over the past couple of years, and now I would walk away.

I prayed about many things, for how long I was not sure; I was at peace though. I had released my burdens and desires to the Lord, and I felt totally within his will and purpose for my life. I had run this particular race, and had been trained for the next one.

As I reflected, I began to realize that in serving others, I too had been greatly served. I didn't work at the shelter to receive blessings or any such thing, my understanding was that I worked there to help others less fortunate than I, in obedience to God's will for my life. But I did get blessed! Not so much with wonderful spiritual highs to take me to beyond the clouds, but with life more abundantly in very practical ways. I had grown in wisdom, integrity, hospitality, character, leadership skills, and the list could go on and on. Not that I became a finished product, but that I had journeyed further from where I had begun.

The amazing reflection that I now received was that the residents had probably been a bigger blessing to me than I had been to them. Such is the mystery of serving others. I felt content that my time at the shelter had been beneficial for many. It was rewarding to reflect on my journey.

I rose from my chair, put my set of house keys on the office desk, and walked out to the kitchen. I washed my mug and placed

Prayer Ending

it on the draining board. I returned to the office to close and lock the door and set the alarm. I quickly exited out of the rear door, closing it behind me and twisting the door handle to test and make sure it was properly locked.

As I walked down the steps, I had this strange sense not to look back. I didn't. I walked to my car and drove home.

With thankfulness, I had left the job God had so wonderfully provided for me. But I also had a sense of excitement. When I first announced I would be resigning from my position, I had no other job to go to, but God had now miraculously provided again. I would be starting my new role as Training and Development Director with Teen Challenge, Brisbane.

www.ingramcontent.com/pod-product-compliance
Lightning Source LLC
Chambersburg PA
CBHW070920160426
43193CB00011B/1539